Inherited
Fate

Inherited Fate

Family Trauma and the Ways of Healing

Noémi Orvos-Tóth

Translated by Katalin Rácz and Thomas Mansell

Cornerstone Press

Cornerstone Press

UK | USA | Canada | Ireland | Australia
India | New Zealand | South Africa

Cornerstone Press is part of the Penguin Random House group of companies
whose addresses can be found at global.penguinrandomhouse.com

Penguin Random House UK,
One Embassy Gardens, 8 Viaduct Gardens, London SW11 7BW

penguin.co.uk
global.penguinrandomhouse.com

Penguin
Random House
UK

First published in Hungary by Helikon/Libri, 2023
First published in the UK in 2025

001

Copyright © Noémi Orvos-Tóth, 2025
Translation © Katalin Rácz and Thomas Mansell, 2025

The moral right of the author has been asserted

Typeset in 13.5/16pt Garamond MT Std by Jouve (UK), Milton Keynes
Printed and bound in India by Manipal Technologies Limited

The authorised representative in the EEA is Penguin Random House Ireland,
Morrison Chambers, 32 Nassau Street, Dublin D02 YH68

A CIP catalogue record for this book is available from the British Library

ISBN: 978–1–529–94131–9 (hardback)
ISBN: 978–1–529–94132–6 (trade paperback)

Penguin Random House is committed to a sustainable future
for our business, our readers and our planet. This book is made
from Forest Stewardship Council® certified paper.

Contents

CONTENTS

PART THREE
Family secrets

PART FOUR
Forming the family's fate

PART FIVE
In the wake of inheritance

Introduction

When someone comes to see me and we start talking about their troubles or recurring negative patterns in their lives, in most cases I soon get the feeling that we need to go back in time.

For some people, this can seem strange or even nonsensical. I well remember a man who came to see me a few years ago who tinkered with his watch while eyeing me distrustfully. His problem was that he kept calling for an ambulance or asking his wife to take him to A&E because he thought he was having a heart attack. Each time, the doctor set his mind at rest, telling him it was a 'false alarm', and sending him off with some advice about changing his way of life – less salt, more exercise, that kind of thing. However, on the latest such occasion, the doctor patted him on the back and said, 'Listen, your heart is completely fine! You should go and see a psychologist instead!' So he came and sat opposite me to find out what might be causing his panic attacks and if anything could be done about them. However, before we could begin, he strictly forbade us from dredging up the past. 'I'm an optimist,' he said. 'I like looking ahead. Let's talk about the future!'

I often encounter similar reservations. Most people

think that it's pointless delving into the past since it cannot be changed. This comes from the conviction that old wounds can only be cured if we rewrite the history of our lives, and since such rewriting is impossible, it's not worth stirring up the past. 'What's done is done' is the often repeated, well-meaning advice. 'Forget about it!' However, that would be a mistake.

It is true that we cannot undo what has happened, but if we understand it, it can help give a different shape to the present and to our future. As Winston Churchill observed, 'The longer back you can look, the further forward you are likely to see.' You must care about the past, because only by understanding it thoroughly can you arm yourself for future challenges.

Of course, it's not always easy to recognise the connections. A sceptic might ask how much events that happened decades ago have to do with our present sufferings. In most cases, however, the answer is 'a lot'.

Some people are unwilling to face the past because they feel they could not cope with some unknown information turning up – of skeletons suddenly falling out of the closet. For example, one of my patients vehemently protested against therapy in an altered state of consciousness – I deliberately don't use the word *hypnosis* as it involves so many misapprehensions – because he was afraid of 'some monstrosity hiding in the depth of [his] unconsciousness'. But this fear consumed far more energy than he would have needed to cope with any potentially surfacing horror. Another characteristic reservation arises from how some people imagine therapy. Many still think that a psychologist acts like a judge, their main task being to assess who is at fault in a given situation and to attribute blame – and they would not like it if it turned out to be them. Recently, a couple began their session by saying that they had come so that I might listen to each of them and then ascertain who was the fool. I had to disappoint them, because as a psychologist I don't have a radar for detecting fools, and anyway I wouldn't like to label anyone. Others actively want to avoid situations where exploring the past would require them to re-evaluate relationships with their relatives. One woman, for example, declared in our very first session that psychologists always blame the mother for everything, whereas her mother was wonderful, so I could forget about her saying anything bad about her. But loyalty to one's family is such a strong dictate that it can literally prevent us from seeing what has happened to us, and from understanding connections in our lives. Let me just say, by the way, that this doesn't only affect lay people. I was once present with a group of people who work in the caring professions who were discussing grievances caused in childhood by parents. It was an upsetting conversation. The next session that day began in complete silence, with no one willing to say anything – until finally someone blurted out their remorse for 'exposing' their parents in the previous session. Even as adults, it can feel like a betrayal if we speak about pain felt in childhood, if we bring up deficiencies and disappointments in the parent–child relationship.

We need to put aside such misgivings. Without exploring the past, we can only dimly surmise who we are and why we lead the precise lives we do. In order to understand ourselves, to find out why we falter, to explore and possibly explain our anxieties, flagging spirits and failures, or to understand why we constantly repeat the script of our unhappy relationships, it is not enough merely to examine our own lives. The experiences, incidents, fears and sufferings of our parents and grandparents, and even ancestors we have never met, influence our fate. If these legacies remain in the concealed corners of the familial unconscious, they will prevent us from living a free life.

It is essential to think of ourselves as part of an extensive social and family network and to discover how many threads the past weaves through our present. We must recognise that if something traumatic happened to one of our ancestors, its effects will be detected in the everyday lives of their descendants, years or even decades later. This is no longer an esoteric view – 'I believe it if I want to' – but a fact backed up by scientific research.

This book invites the reader on a journey of self-awareness that spans generations. It encourages you to be brave and to explore your family's long-buried stories, to set off on densely overgrown paths, cast light in dark corners, and face the forces that are at work in your life. I am convinced that no one's fate can be fully understood without taking into account transgenerational influences, and that if you explore your ancestors' history you can discover the key to positive change.

At the end of each chapter, I have collected some questions, the answers to which can help us to develop our self-awareness more thoroughly. They may take us closer to the hidden layers of the self and clarify our parents' and grandparents' behaviour and emotional reactions, as well as their decisions.

PART ONE
How it began

The baby suffers as well
When the mother is giving birth:
A double pain – only humility can ease it.

Attila József, 'It Hurts a Lot'[1]

The drama of the unwanted child

But you were born
And you're neither blind nor a fool;
Once you're here,
Don't let them stop you short!
Péter Sziámi Müller, 'If you'd been
a baby with foresight'[2]

As a child in the 1970s and 1980s, I remember listening a lot to songs by the popular Hungarian singer Zsuzsa Koncz. We would sing along with her as the black vinyl spun round on the record player. 'Mama, kérlek' ('Please, Mum') was my favourite: I still get goose pimples when I hear János Bródy's brilliant lyrics. Great artists – poets, writers or lyricists – know as much about the human soul as a psychologist, if not more, but they approach things from a different angle. 'Mama, kérlek' put into words life's fundamental question, singing 'I never asked you to give me life,' and asking that before she die 'I need to know why I'm alive.'

Why are we here? For what purpose were we born? Did my parents want me? In the 1980s, when the song came out, I had no idea how often I'd be searching for answers to such questions in my work as a psychologist.

As soon as therapy begins, I try to discover what my clients know about the events surrounding their conception. Who were their parents? What was their relationship like? What kind of lives did they lead? Were they looking forward to the birth or was it a mistake, an accident? Was the child born following an unplanned pregnancy, which can be something of a burden? Ideally, a child arrives in the world thanks to the deep commitment and mutual desire of two mature adults who love each other and who are emotionally and financially secure, yet life doesn't always spoil us with such ideal scenarios.

Why is our conception such an important topic? How does what happens at the very beginning of our lives affect our future?

Our early development takes place in the interaction between our genes and the environment, and the very first environment we encounter is our mother's body. For a long time it was thought that the only growth that took place in the womb was physical, but thanks to modern research into infancy, and in particular to ultrasound tests, it has become clear that very important developmental processes, about which we previously knew little, also take place there. The embryo is alert, listening, responding, and above all *learning*. Its immature nervous system stores experiences. The maternal body not only provides nutrition but also passes on the mother's emotional state of mind: if the mother feels good, the embryo also swims in happiness hormones, whereas if she is tense and nervous the embryo also receives her stress hormones. These biochemical messages change into memory imprints, which are stored in the form of physical feelings and visceral impressions. We are not talking about conscious memories that can be put into words, but rather experiences at a cellular level.

Examining the influence of the mother's body on the embryo, Vivette Glover, professor of perinatal psychology at Imperial College London, claims that a mother's emotional state affects the development of the embryo's nervous system. If the mother is stressed, the increased levels of cortisol can cause structural and functional changes in the embryo's brain, detected mostly in the region known as the hippocampus. Situated in both cerebral hemispheres, roughly behind the temples, and somewhat resembling a seahorse (*hippocampus* in Latin), this region is primarily responsible for learning and memory and also for the regulation of emotions and motivation. Research by Glover and others has proved that due to the different development of their nervous systems, children of mothers with depression and anxiety are more likely to go on to suffer symptoms of depression and anxiety themselves; they are also more likely to have attention deficit disorders, learning difficulties and cognitive problems. Stress endured as an embryo may affect someone's whole life and fate. Scientific research now supports the advice given by Aristotle more than two thousand years ago, when he warned pregnant women against worrying on the basis that the baby developing in their womb absorbs a great deal, just as a plant does from the soil in which it is growing.

Some aspects of becoming a mother are not considered fit topics for discussion, and often we dare not talk about them for fear that some people may find the whole truth shocking. It is commonly assumed that every woman awaits the birth of her baby with exuberant joy, and if someone – even only in a passing moment, or in certain periods of her pregnancy – feels anything other than this, she exposes herself to others' angry disapproval. The late Hungarian psychologist Péter Popper, who, for me, was one of the most intrepid and insightful explorers of the human soul, asked whether it was true that every father and mother loves their child, discussing it in the following way:

Psychologists' surgeries are full of broken or breaking relationships, because people dutifully pretend to love their children at all times and under any circumstances. It is a social obligation! What kind of a monster of a mother or father doesn't love their own child! However, it is perfectly possible to care properly for a child and treat it with kindness (for example, for the sake of decency or goodwill, or out of a sense of responsibility) even if one does not love the child but accepts the situation – those are the cards life has dealt you.[3]

International surveys echo Popper's words, with results showing that 56 per cent of couples react to a positive pregnancy test with fear. Of course, in most cases, the initial shock dissipates, yet more pregnancies than we might like to think are accompanied with negative emotions. According to one American study, more than one third (!) of children are born from unwanted pregnancies, even though contraceptive pills and condoms are widely available in Western societies. However, sweet-sounding principles are significantly different from practice in this field, too. (In its annual report for 2022, the UN Population Fund refers to a neglected crisis in unwanted pregnancies, which affects not only the individual, but society as a whole.[4])

But what must the situation have been like before the 1960s, when contraception was harder to procure and abortion was illegal? I think we can venture that in every generation significant numbers of babies came into the world whose parents had not wanted them at all. One of my patients comes to mind. Her mother often told her, 'If you hadn't been born, my life would have been different. I wouldn't be rotting away in this damned marriage with your dad.' No wonder it wasn't easy for her to have a satisfying relationship; she simply did not believe that anyone needed her or that anyone would approach her with love.

As early as 1929, the renowned Hungarian psychoanalyst Sándor Ferenczi, a disciple of Freud, considered how a mother's rejection affected a child. In his study

'The Unwelcome Child and his Death-Instinct',[5] Ferenczi claims that there is a destructive instinct, the 'death instinct', in every embryo, and that maternal love is able to reduce and calm its harmful power. If our mother thinks of us lovingly, it makes our existence worthwhile and gives us purpose. However, if pregnancy is not a joy for her, if our mother radiates rejection towards us and this persists, it makes our beginning difficult. The death instinct is not counterbalanced, and life is imbued with feelings of insecurity and distrust. This situation may improve later if there is at least one other person in our environment with a positive image of us. But if there is no such person, the possibility of having really deep and harmonious relationships becomes much more difficult.

Ferenczi thought that unwanted children developed more slowly, that they would become oversensitive and pessimistic as well as more inclined to psychosomatic maladies. He believed these to be manifestations of the death instinct, a kind of unconscious tendency towards self-destruction. According to Ferenczi, as adults unwanted children are more susceptible to suicide and criminal inclinations, as though someone whose existence was unwelcome would be more inclined to self-harm, as if satisfying the parental expectation. It is worth repeating that this study was published in 1929. For nearly a century, therefore, psychologists have been concerned with the possible consequences if the animating power of love is absent from the very first relationship of our lives.

In *Ungewollte Kinder* (*Unwanted Children*),[6] Helga Häsing and Ludwig Janus write that if the mother wanted the pregnancy the embryo would develop in a 'blissful primal state', whereas if she rejected it, the child would develop a very deep, archaic guilty conscience. They would unconsciously feel that they are doing something wrong, and therefore try to annihilate themselves. In *Rainbow States of Consciousness*,[7] Andrew Feldmár talks about his experience of working with patients who survived multiple attempts at suicide. He found that several of them always tried to end their lives in the same month of the year and, analysing his patients' lifelines, Feldmár realised that each suicide attempt took place during the period corresponding to the three months following their conception, the so-called first trimester – the period when unwanted pregnancies are usually terminated. He decided to talk to his patients' mothers and ask them whether they had tried to have an abortion: it turned out that all of the mothers would have liked to have ended their pregnancy. Although these are individual cases, they still make one think. How is this gruesome coincidence possible when the young people concerned had no information about those past events? Could they somehow 'remember' the threatening experience during foetal life? Did the mother's emotions and thoughts reach them via an invisible channel of communication? Did they identify with the aggression directed at them and, having grown up, try to harm themselves? It's possible – but then how can we explain the coincidence in time? Prominent psychotherapist Anne Ancelin Schützenberger thought that the 'anniversary syndrome' might lie behind this – the phenomenon whereby anniversaries of incidents that happened to an ancestor or significant events in their lives (for example, an accident or a death) could have a magnetic force and evoke repetitions.

In recent decades, several surveys have examined what happens when the earliest bond between mother and child is damaged. The 'Prague Study'[8] by David, Matějček and Dytrych is perhaps the most famous of these. The researchers followed 220 children for the first thirty-five years of their lives, all of whom had been born despite their mothers having applied for abortions (appearing twice before the relevant committee between 1961 and 1963). The authors wanted to understand how this clear and open rejection affected the children's future lives. The results showed the importance of the emotions expressed towards us since our conception. Although unwanted children were no different in their intellectual abilities (IQ) from their peers, they were poor achievers in several subjects compared to those in the control group who were wanted in pregnancy. They lagged behind in their social skills, they fitted into the community with more difficulty, and they were the children their peers were reluctant to make friends with – as if maternal rejection returned in their later human relationships. Their teachers and mothers were dissatisfied with their behaviour and diligence, and so they came to be labelled 'bad children'. These early classifications are deeply engraved in the image we form of ourselves. The negative adjectives heard in our childhood can accompany us even to the end of life. Children of unwanted pregnancies had problems regulating their emotions and found it harder to control their temper. As adults, almost twice as many became alcoholics and nearly three times as many committed crimes compared with the members of the control group. Many of them thought that they struggled in vain for acceptance and that however much they tried to accomplish something, things would always go wrong. 'Even my mother didn't love me: there must be something wrong with me,' they must have thought. If someone's soul is filled with feelings of worthlessness, it's no wonder that as adults they will start any relationship feeling insecure and afraid, or refuse to let anyone close to avoid being further wounded. For such a person, love becomes a mirage: they either pursue it in despair or sometimes don't even bother. So perhaps understandably the unwanted children in the Prague Study experienced much disappointment and failure, and many break-ups in their relationships as adults. Their first sexual encounters (which generally determine the quality of future relationships) were usually superficial, and their later affairs also tended to be fleeting or short-lived. They offered their bodies almost automatically for temporary kindness and the illusion of love, but were not able to form deep and lasting bonds.

Several felt unhappy in their marriages, and they were more likely to get divorced.

An initial lack of love acts like a thread that runs through our lives and it is difficult to unpick. Having once been unwanted in this world, we struggle ever to believe that we have a place in it, that we are owed honour and acceptance and can experience real, deep intimacy. Of course, this rarely comes to the surface: what we notice instead is that we repeatedly falter, our relationships go awry, we lose hope, nothing excites us, or we lead a self-destructive life.

Recently I noticed a homeless person sitting on a bench near where I live. He was there in the morning when I went to work and still there when I returned home in the evening, sitting peacefully, listening to his radio. One morning when I saw him in the same place, I spoke to him. He told me that he had lived on the street since 1994. He had lost his job when the factory where he had been working closed down. Rather than try to look for work elsewhere, he simply gave up because he didn't think it was worth striving for anything or that his actions would ever achieve a positive outcome. The long and the short of it was that the man was an unwanted child. 'My parents never wanted me: for them, I was just a pain in the arse,' he said, with a dismissive gesture.

When we cannot comprehend someone's 'laziness' and 'lack of motivation', it is worth casting an eye over the life they have experienced so far. How many people had given up on them by the time they gave up on themselves?

But how does being 'unwanted' have an effect even across several generations? Mark Wolynn, an expert on inherited family traumas, says that aspects of our grandmother's maternal care are passed on to us. Our grandmother's childhood sorrows, difficulties and sufferings influenced how she later treated our mother, and our mother in turn passed these influences on to us. If we don't manage the trauma of rejection, we pass it on like a hot potato to our children, and they to our grandchildren.

In a group session, Ágota, a softly spoken, reserved woman in her fifties, complains of apathy and being tired of life. She drags herself along sorrowfully from one day to another and no longer expects or wants anything. She says the struggle of constantly trying to live up to expectations has exhausted her. Her motivation has petered out, she does not want to know the future. 'Life for me has been used up,' she says, and whoever sees her cannot doubt it. Her body has been drained of energy: her lips curve downwards, her shoulders droop forward, and her eyes bespeak utter weariness. She herself does not understand why she is like this: after all, she has a husband who loves her and a daughter who is doing well; she has a job, a nice house and a garden. On paper, at least, she has everything she needs to be happy; the soul, however, couldn't care less.

In my work, I have observed that emotions often erupt seemingly without warning or explanation. We look for the catalyst, but even if we find something, we somehow don't feel it's the whole picture. At such moments, it's a good idea to dig a bit deeper and conduct a search into our ancestors.

Ágota and I begin treating the matter on a transgenerational level. She draws up her family tree and searches archives and church documents for faded papers. She comes across some interesting information in a church register of births, a remark after her mother's name: illegitimate. How could this be? She had never heard anything about this before. Her mother is no longer alive so cannot be asked, but Ágota doesn't give up. She puts questions to members of the family until at last a relative tells her the story she wants to know. Her grandparents were teenagers when they fell in love. They were in the grip of passion and, presumably knowing little about contraception, the fifteen-year-old girl became pregnant. She only found out when she started to feel the baby move. A huge scandal broke out in the village and everyone talked about the girl who had lost her honour. Her parents, who were unsociable and loveless people, utterly humiliated her and threatened to disown her. She had to move out to the stables and was given hardly anything to eat. The young couple applied to marry with an exemption from the age of consent, but the baby was born before the permission arrived. This was the cause of illegitimacy.

Later, when they got married, they made the child 'legitimate', yet that only resolved the legalities. The child (Ágota's mother), who came unexpectedly and too early, was the target of aggressive emotions all her life. Every move she made was criticised. Rare indeed were the days that she was not scolded or thrashed. (Research also shows that unwanted children suffer far more abuse in their family, which they pass on to their own children: several investigations into the frequency of transgenerational transfer have confirmed that about a third of formerly abused children will themselves become abusing parents.) So Ágota's mother grew up in that traumatising environment and could never shake off her memories. The childhood pattern of damage stubbornly persisted: the abused girl became an abusing mother. As a result, Ágota also suffered in her childhood: sometimes she was hurt by words, sometimes beaten with a belt. When she remembers those years, she cannot recall many cheerful moments. She says she did nothing but try to meet expectations and appease her constantly angry, emotionally rigid and rejecting mother, with little success. Even as a young girl she had to run the entire household. She washed the clothes, cleaned the house, fed the animals, and made jam in the summer. Every day she dreaded what mistake her mother was going to pick on. She decided that once she grew up she was going to flee, to go somewhere far away and to do her best to avoid becoming like her mother.

Ágota more or less managed to keep her pledge: in fact, she moved to the other end of the country. She met a steady, intelligent man and she told him about her childhood. He realised that living in Ágota's soul was an abused little girl who, from time to time, had to be treated gently, with empathy. When their child was born, Ágota found that her anger sometimes rose when the baby was crying. In those moments it was as if her mother's spirit replaced hers. She feared that one day she would lose control of herself and destroy the child. Ágota and her husband agreed that if he saw signs of tension in her, he would immediately remove the baby so she could not hurt her. This was the 'trick' for her not to pass on the transgenerational pattern and not make her own daughter a victim. It proved effective and their daughter grew up in a more or less harmonious atmosphere. Now grown, she had been living and working abroad for a year, and because of the distance she and Ágota could only stay in touch on Skype. And here something interesting comes to light: Ágota's depression began more or less when it became clear to her that her daughter would now only come home as a visitor. Although she was sure that her daughter was getting on well, she felt destroyed by losing her. 'She doesn't want me either!' an inner voice whispered. 'My mother didn't want me, and now neither does my daughter!' She was struck by a dreadful pain, which was later replaced by indifference and resignation.

In groupwork, we return to her childhood experiences and start working on the feelings of rejection she has carried since then. We role-play the inner drama of her relationship with her mother and, with the help of the others, she re-enacts the terrible scenes she experienced as a little girl. Correction can come after that. Acceptance, support, invigorating love – all are included in her desires, and we are there to help her experience what was absent from her childhood. We hold and embrace her, and she is slowly able to allow herself to be in this unknown feeling.

Later, when she is thinking about her relationship with her mother, she suddenly sees her in a different light. She realises that until now she regarded her only as the mother who gave birth to her, and never as the defenceless child who had been treated cruelly at the hands of others. As she recognises and feels the significance of her mother's pain as a child, Ágota begins to cry. She feels sorry for that little girl. All her life she's been looking for the thread that could bond her to her mother and at last she's found it: their shared experience was the lack of love, the feeling of being hurt and rejected. Ágota's pain and anger is slowly being replaced by sympathy and then forgiveness. Her joy for life seems to return in the following weeks and, although she hardly notices, she becomes more active and lively again. Her daughter's departure is thought of differently. She no longer sees her as walking out on her, but as exercising independence, which Ágota is even able to be happy about.

Another memorable case in my practice concerned a woman in her forties. Her persistent panic attacks seemed to be getting worse and worse over the years. By then the situation had got so bad that she had to cancel her most recent business trip because even the thought of boarding a plane made her run to the bathroom retching. Nevertheless, everything was fine – at least that's what she said. Her professional career was of the type that most people wouldn't even dream of. She lived in a villa in Buda and had exotic holidays. Her relationship with her husband could be called good, although they did not have much time for each other because of work. Her daughter was studying abroad at university. She said she was not sentimental, had no time to whine and had got used to gritting her teeth if she wanted to achieve something. She was always driven to prove herself, and ever since childhood accomplishment was of the utmost importance to her. Her life was precisely planned. She managed and controlled everything she could. Only the wretched panic attacks thwarted her. It began when she started to feel strangely tense in large shopping centres. Later, she took taxis whenever she could because the inexplicable fear kept overwhelming her while driving. It was hard to breathe properly, she felt dizzy, shivered, and sweated profusely. In order to avoid these unpleasant and harassing experiences, she excluded an increasing number of situations from her life, even if it put her job at risk.

She had to fly in four weeks' time. She was due to be the keynote speaker at an international conference she couldn't fail to attend. She urgently needed a technique to be able to handle her tension. She did not want to talk about her past and her family – there was no time for that. 'Let's manage the symptoms: that's more than enough,' she said. We started to work more intensively and established the hierarchy of her fears. She learned to relax and in that calm condition she imagined she was packing and setting off for the airport. Each session brought us closer to the most fearful moment of take-off. When the journey came it was relatively successful; her anxiety could be held in check. That's that, she thought, she'd achieved what she needed, so we said goodbye.

Three weeks later she called on me again. She was restless, unable to focus on her job. She had had yet another rather serious panic attack. She couldn't pinpoint a cause for feeling so wretched. Her attention was mostly occupied by her current state, and she couldn't find any relief from the problems of 'the here and now'. Whichever direction I led her in during our sessions, she always returned to her symptoms. But we kept talking and then on one occasion she blurted out how unhappy her father had been about her birth. She was the fourth child and her conception was unexpected. Her parents were not planning to have another child, and her father just couldn't accept that it was all going to start all over again. She didn't remember much about her childhood, but, however much she might want to, she couldn't forget that whenever she got in a muddle or had a weak report at school her father simply shook his head and said, 'What a pity, what a pity' – meaning a pity that she had been born. In order never to hear these painful words, she did her utmost to maximise her potential. She studied hard and constantly pushed herself because she wanted to prove that her existence was not 'a pity'. She lost her parents early, so neither was alive when she became successful in her profession. For many years, her life was focused on achievement, and she attributed her recurring panic attacks to overwork. When I asked her when she had had her first panic attack, she couldn't recall. Only later did she remember that it was when she sold her parents' house in the country, which had been empty for years. Before she had handed over the keys to the buyer, she spent a day there packing up old things. She says it was like time travel. She was standing in the kitchen as she had done long ago, when she suddenly heard anew her father's voice. The painful memories struck her powerfully. She cried her eyes out as if a dam had burst in her. All the success and all the effort had been in vain: she was not wanted in the world. After she had cried her heart out, she once again banished these painful feelings from her mind and pretended that nothing had happened. She was taken ill for the first time a few days later. The doctor on duty comforted her, saying she was not going to die because she had 'only' had a panic attack, not a heart attack. Since then the attacks had become more frequent and severe, disrupting what she considered most important: her work.

I thought it was worth retuning her attitude to the

panic attacks. I encouraged her to see them as eccentric but well-intentioned friends who would nudge her when they thought her life was not going in the right direction. If she tried to bottle up the pain she'd suppressed since childhood, a panic attack would come along and rebuke her. Since she wouldn't listen, this symptom of her anxiety was unwilling to go.

So how could she get rid of her anxiety? What did she have to do? She must acknowledge, express and process the fact that she was not wanted, and then realise how much she had been doing to get her parents to see that her birth *was*, after all, worthwhile. Throughout her life she had sought approval, and she had suppressed her feelings, chasing success and accomplishing so much in order to win a place in her parents' hearts. To get rid of the panic attacks once and for all, she didn't just need an effective technique for managing them: she also had to give space to her feelings and to find a balance between reason and emotion. Anger, disappointment, shame, a fear of loneliness, and a desperate desire to be loved – these feelings were seething in her, yet she never dared face them. She was angry at her parents for rejecting her. She was disappointed and ashamed because she thought that if even those who gave her life weren't happy to have her, something must be wrong with her. When she eventually acknowledged the emotions she had previously denied, she realised how much she dreaded loneliness and how strongly she wanted to be loved. She realised, too, that she was reserved and cool in her relationship with her own daughter and with her husband because that was how she protected herself from disappointment (should it turn out that they did not love her either). Working late and being constantly on the go wasn't itself joyful, but was, rather, a kind of defence against intimacy. Therapy not only brought about a change in her but had an effect on the quality of her relationships. She talked to her daughter and husband at length, and in turn they expressed how much it upset them that she always prioritised her career. Moreover, this was precisely why her daughter also tried to gain *her* love with outstanding achievements, involuntarily continuing her legacy. Their conversations helped the daughter's own compulsion to comply and excel.

Transgenerational self-awareness can be assisted by answering the following questions:

— *What do you know about the circumstances of your conception?*
— *Was your conception wanted by both your parents?*
— *Were you a desired and wanted child?*
— *How did your grandparents receive the news of your imminent arrival?*
— *How did your other relatives respond?*
— *Did anyone receive the news of your arrival with worry or antipathy?*
— *How did your family prepare for your birth?*

— *Do your parents and your family have any stories about the period immediately before you were born? (For example: 'When I was pregnant with you, I couldn't even look at fish and chips, but had huge cravings for lemon sorbet.')*

— *Did they tell you anything about your time in the womb? (For example: 'You were already restless even in my belly.') These stories reveal a lot about ideas your mother formed about you.*

— *What do you know about the circumstances of your birth? Where and how did it happen? Who was present? Is there an often-repeated story about that time?*

— *Do you know any stories about when you were a baby or a toddler?*

— *Have the family kept photos, objects or mementos from when you were a baby or a toddler (first lock of hair, baby shoes, clothes, toys)?*

What a pity it's a boy/girl!

> In the end, I just wished to be myself:
> An old, unhappy, self-centred creature,
> who is searching for a meaning,
> a reason for being in the world.
> and why am I a boy and not a girl.
>
> György Petri, 'Simple, songlike'[9]

In a certain sense, our life begins long before conception. The early fantasies of your parents-to-be imply expectations projected towards the future and reveal much about the years ahead. 'I'll have two daughters. I'll name them Isabella and Sonia,' a teenage girl says, totally convinced. 'This is where I played football; one day, I'll bring my son here too,' says a young man, pointing proudly at the club's playing grounds. But what happens if things turn out differently? If a boy is born when a girl was expected, or a baby girl appears when the parents wanted a baby boy? How does this affect the life of the child?

In one of his lectures Péter Popper talked about his own life and about how, though his mother always wanted the best for him and treated him well, she was unable to open up to him and he struggled to open up to her. 'She would say, "Come on, Pete, let's talk! Sit on my lap till your dad comes home!" I just couldn't do it, and I didn't know why. Something simply did not work, mood- and emotion-wise.' Popper revealed how, when he was in his late thirties, his cousin had had a stillborn child and Popper's mother had tried, in her own way, to console the grieving woman, telling her that she had always prayed for a girl child. She didn't like boys and after her son, Péter, was born, she never wanted to be pregnant again. Popper described how, in the very moment his cousin revealed this to him, he suddenly understood the problem of confidence in his relationship with his mother.

What awful trouble I had caused to this poor mother who in no way wanted a boy! From that point on, all aversion in me was relieved, and we got on very well until her death. I'm ever so grateful for my cousin's loose tongue, because until then I could only sense that something between us did not add up. I needed that secret nugget to understand my own feelings and explain why I could not be close to my mother and why even in adulthood it remained so crucial for me to be accepted by women.[10]

It is not a unique story. It is never easy for a child who does not meet their parents' requirements, if one or both parents only wanted a child of another gender.

A woman in her fifties with a harrowed look comes to see me. She tells me how bleak her life is. She has no partner, no children; she lives alone. Her periods stopped in her twenties and she was diagnosed with premature ovarian insufficiency. 'My femininity had run out, although I was never very feminine before that either,' she smiles bitterly. When I ask her why not, she says her father expected a boy and could never overcome his disappointment when she was born a girl. He regularly remarked that girls were useless. That they were nothing but trouble. How much better it would have been if they'd had a boy. And he treated her as if she were a boy: though she longed for a swirly dress and tap shoes, she was only allowed trousers and trainers. Similarly, it was futile for her to crave a doll: all her parents bought her were boys' toys. Her father didn't let her grow her hair either. Every other week he himself cut it so it was barely half an inch long. He brought a shabby little stool to the middle of the kitchen and she had to cower there while her father did the job. She was called Buddy,* and the nickname

---

* Translators' note: it is difficult to find an English equivalent for the Hungarian word *Öcsi* – a common term of endearment used, for example, by the whole nation to refer to the legendary footballer Ferenc Puskás (1927–2006).

stuck – at first only within the family, but later with classmates and friends too. Everywhere she went, people thought she was a boy, and she didn't dare say (much as she would have liked to), 'Hi, there: I'm a girl!' Because of her 'wrong' sex, she felt she had committed a crime – one that she couldn't remedy in any way. She was right about that; despite her early menopause, she was still a woman.

I suggest that we try Imago Therapy (from the Latin for 'copy' or 'likeness'). In Imago Therapy, the stimuli of the outside world lose their significance as an intensive inner attention is formed. Clients call up images, feelings and symbols from their unconscious while in a meditative, relaxed state. During the process, imprints of painful memories of the past are replaced by healing images. Over time, the brain will receive these new images as reality and the power of traumatic events can be reduced.

I ask her to recall the past image of her hair being cut, to allow her body to remember and experience what she felt at the time. Then she can enter the scene as an adult and do what the little girl could not yet do: stand up for herself. She imagines going up to her father, taking his hand, and putting a stop to this psychologically painful haircut. She tells him to stop abusing his daughter, because for her it's as if he was harming her, depriving her of an important attribute of her femininity. Then she turns to herself as a little girl, pulling her close, embracing her, rocking and comforting her. She asks her to set her mind at rest and to have the courage to protest if something happens to her in the future that she doesn't want.

This very powerful inner cinema is the first to draw her away from the basic position of 'I'm guilty because I wasn't born a boy'. Of course, the therapy is far from being over. Lasting and deep transformations are not achieved so easily. The earlier an injury is inflicted, the longer it usually takes to draw forth and overwrite these deeply encoded patterns, relations and beliefs.

My client's case is far from rare. In fact, you'd hardly believe how widespread gender disappointment is. For example, the UN estimates that 200 million girls are 'missing' from the world – girls whose parents got rid of them because of their sex. In cultures where girls are still endowed for large sums of money, a female child represents a significant financial burden for a family. 'Pay 5,000 rupees today to save 50,000 tomorrow,' some Indian doctors advertise, hinting that an abortion, while expensive, is still cheaper than a wedding dowry. Although sex-selective abortion is against the law, many couples still opt for an illegal abortion if the embryo is female. (This has other catastrophic social consequences too: in India, for example, eligible men outnumber single women, so many have little chance of finding a wife. In many places, men experience the lack or absence of women as a famine, which forecasts increasing social tension and the spread of violence.)

We might like to think that this problem is alien to our culture, but unfortunately it is not so: it happens all over the world. For example, about ten years ago, secret footage emerged of doctors in the UK talking about how often they had terminated pregnancies solely because the embryo's sex did not meet the parents' requirements. Consequently, some hospitals prohibited parents from learning the sex of their baby in the first trimester (when abortion was still possible).

Most people answer the question whether they want a boy or a girl by saying, 'I don't care, as long as the baby is healthy' – and yet within a few minutes of conversation, preferences emerge ('I've always wanted a girl', 'when my son is born . . .' and so on). If we keep our eyes and ears open, the influence of our surroundings becomes obvious. A father announces the birth of his third daughter to friends. 'Well, I don't envy you, mate!' his friends say with a sympathetic pat on the shoulder. Men rile each other: 'A real man makes a boy first! After that, a girl may come!' A preference regarding the sex of a child often implies a very strong expectation, and if you don't meet your parents' expectations you may be at odds with your gender identity throughout your life.

The late Endre Czeizel, a well-known physician, geneticist and broadcaster, was bombarded by couples asking how they could influence the sex of their future child. Today, hundreds of articles recommend techniques which increase the chances of having a baby of the required sex. 'Drink coffee twenty minutes before making love and you'll have a son'; 'Reduce your calorie intake and you'll have a daughter'. And I could list at length all manner of notions regarding the timing and various positions of sexual intercourse. Why are so many articles written about this? Because the demand for them is high. In the Western world, anxious parents often think that if they had a child of their preferred sex, it may be easier to have a good relationship with the child and manage his or her behaviour. 'Boys are wild and aggressive. I don't think I'd feel strong enough to control my child if I had a boy,' says one expectant mother – from which one can see that it is not really the sex of the child but the feeling of parental ineptitude that causes the problem. 'I wouldn't be a good mother to a boy, but I would be to a girl.' This feeling has already been described as *gender disappointment*. Plenty of scientific articles and forums deal with the topic, while professionals try to help parents to accept their children's sex with psychotherapy, supportive talks, and information.

It is important to mention the therapeutic method developed in the mid-1990s by two great Hungarian psychoanalysts, Dr Jenő Raffai and Dr György Hidas. The essence of their mother–child bonding analysis is that the bonding begins before birth (in the 'prenatal realm'). Fewer complications arise in the case of bonding-analysed babies, and the future mother-and-child relationship is also more harmonious. Raffai and his colleagues are convinced that it is important to concern ourselves with the earliest social experiences in life, since everything that happens in the adult world – how we treat others in our relationships, friendships, workplaces, or in the street – reaches back to our childhood. At the same time, early effects are passed on through several generations, so what is happening to our children will even affect our grandchildren.

Questions:

- *Would your family have wanted you to be a boy or a girl?*
- *How did they relate to your sex?*
- *Have you ever had negative feedback about being a boy or a girl?*
- *If there had been any aversion to your sex, was it openly stated or were you made to feel it without words?*
- *Were you allowed to play with boyish/girlish toys?*
- *What remarks and qualifying attributes did your parents make or use about the other gender?*
- *How satisfied are you with your birth sex?*
- *Have you ever put into words that you'd rather have been born another sex?*

Function children

Nothing exerts a stronger psychic effect
upon the human environment, and
especially upon children, than the life
which the parents have not lived.
Carl Gustav Jung, 'Paracelsus'[11]

A 42-year-old woman comes to see me. She is single – and lonely – and has not had more than a few brief relationships in her life. She is shy, reserved, and feels unable to mix with strangers. Her self-confidence is unstable: on several occasions, she has refused promotion because she does not believe in herself. Although she does not emphasise it, I notice that these job offers were either work opportunities abroad or posts which would have required longer regular business trips. The woman, let's call her Anna, seems a fully functioning adult to the superficial observer – she has her own apartment, she earns a good living – yet something is not right. As we get into details and she tells me how she spends her time, it turns out that she has remained 'her parents' little girl'. She spends the majority of her free time with her parents: after work she goes 'home' to them.

They have dinner together, watch TV, and she only leaves late in the evening, to go and sleep in her own apartment. At weekends, they go hiking in the hills and visit relatives; they also spend their holidays together. What would happen if she eased up a little on this close relationship? She cannot even imagine it. As we discuss this possibility, she becomes increasingly tense — but she is also curious. The following weekend, she gives it a try. She cancels Sunday lunch, citing a work event. However, her mother detects something amiss in her voice and does not believe her. On Sunday afternoon she receives a desperate phone call from her mother: her parents have had a big row, her father has stormed off, and her mother does not know where he is. Anna immediately gets into her car and races there — in her own words, 'like an ambulance speeding to a mass casualty incident to try to save lives'. 'What do you think you're saving?' I ask her. She thinks for a long time before answering. Her voice is quiet and hollow: my parents' marriage, she answers. Memories, emotions and pain begin to surface. Something her father once said comes to her mind: 'You were our last trial. If you had not been born, your mother and I would certainly not be together.' So this was the appointed task, the role they assigned to her from birth: she was to be the lightning conductor for her parents, the saviour of their relationship. Of course, she was not consciously aware of what she was doing, but she watched their moods assiduously. She ironed out contradictions, drew attention away from conflicts, and kept her parents' marriage together.

Now in her forties, it is still the great mission of her life – and she does not see why she is single. 'What would happen to your parents if you weren't?' I ask her, and can see her giving it careful thought. She tries to explain it to me, but she is mostly trying to convince herself with what seem to her to be rational reasons: her parents will soon need to be cared for; she is the only one they can rely on. The outcome of her thoughts is, again, that she must carry on: there is no way she can abandon her task of being by her parents' side.

When I suggest that she does not seem to be beside them but between them, she is surprised and does not understand the difference. To help her see the situation better, we take three chairs which symbolise her and her parents. I ask her to arrange them as they are now. She places the three chairs close to one another with hers in the middle. She tests one after the other what it is like to sit on the chairs, and is astonished to see that in fact no one has any space: her parents can only reach each other through her and if she wants to see one of them, she has to turn to the left or right. 'I have to turn my back on either my mother or my father,' she says. I ask her to arrange the chairs in a better way. After some thought, she picks up the middle chair and places it a bit further away, facing the 'parents'. Like this, she can see both of them easily and they can connect directly with each other. Then, with a careful movement, she turns her chair somewhat, away from the parents, for she would like to see other things too, not just them. Past forty, she is slowly opening up to the world.

Before we are born, our parents may set various tasks for us. In Anna's case, for example, it was to salvage their crumbling marriage, to give their relationship a sense of meaning and purpose. Other parents expect their children to make their dreams come true, to achieve what they didn't manage to, or perhaps they use their children as companions to save them from loneliness. Consider to what extent it is about the parents or their children. The stronger the ideas parents have about what their children must do, the more tasks they intend for their children, the less opportunity the children have to choose freely. Of course, parents usually think that they only want what's best for their children, and it rarely occurs to them that their child might not necessarily be of the same opinion. What success or happiness means in their lives may present itself as the opposite for the child. A dull, unfulfilled life is often caused by nothing other than a sense of obligation to follow a path different from one's own.

By the time a child is born, its parents have accumulated countless frustrations: goals they didn't achieve, dreams that didn't come true, and plans that fell through. Even if they have succeeded in life, as the years go by, their failures may make them nostalgic, and often seem to weigh more than what has been realised. If they cannot get over this, if they really do not understand that these are their own personal wishes and failures, they might use their children to experience vicariously something that they didn't. 'We wanted that for ourselves because it is good,' they reason, 'and what's good (or would have been good) for us will be good for our children.' And they begin to push their children in the 'right direction', sometimes gently, sometimes with force.

A member of a dynasty of doctors told me that he hadn't the slightest intention of choosing that profession: what interested him was philosophy, and ever since he was a teenager he'd wanted to write and teach. Of course, the family wouldn't hear of it. After all, as they'd told him repeatedly since he was a child, he was born to take up the baton. Every member of the family in their own way tried to convince him to sit the entrance exam for medical school. His father shouted, his mother took to her bed to demonstrate how their son's disobedience was wearing her down, while his grandfather, the founder of the dynasty, responded with silent rejection. Under such pressure, the only possible option was to give in. The man is now fifty. He hates life and the very idea of hospital makes him shiver. He doesn't have a profession, only a job, and he regards his life as a treadmill from which there is no escape. At night he tosses and turns, unable to sleep, and imagines how he would be now if he had dared fight for his dream.

As I listened to him, the saying about the road to

hell being paved with good intentions came to mind. This man's parents and grandparents were absolutely sure they were doing good for their son and grandson. For them, a career in medicine meant social advancement, an excellent standard of living, trips abroad, and a wide social network. They tried to pass it all on to him. Behind their aggression was a conviction that 'we know how to get on in life – after all, we've done it'. They had no faith in the son's inner compass to point him in the right direction nor in his ability to choose his own profession – nor did they believe that without their social contacts he would be able to make it in life. They clung tenaciously to their own conceptions, because for them that meant security. Life seemed predictable and manageable in that way. There was no negative intention on their part. Parents generally try to pass on to their children the life strategies they think may help them. If in an insecure world – and the twentieth century in which they had lived most of their lives was certainly that – they had managed to earn a secure living and achieve a good social position, then they were inclined to force their child, even aggressively, to do what they thought was right.

The documentary series *Toddlers and Tiaras* reveals the lives of function children with terrible clarity. Offering an insight into the world of American child beauty pageants, in every episode you see obsessed mothers trying to realise their own dreams via their children's lives, dragging their tiny tots to shows across the USA. The youngest 'competitors' are still in nappies – not only do these children not benefit from the experience, they are undoubtedly harmed by all the fuss and commotion. In interviews, the mothers reveal that they themselves had participated in child beauty contests when younger, but as they aged they were unable to continue in the beauty industry, or they never won parts in shows even though they always wanted to shine onstage. The mothers' frustration turned into their children's fate.

The saddest part for me was when a little boy was sprayed with self-tan and had his hair fixed with gel while his mother explained what a pity it was that she 'only' had a son. All she could do was take him along to the pageants; how much better it would be to experience the contests with a little girl who could be clothed in pretty dresses!

We may all be tempted to shape our children's lives as we imagine them. Before they are even born, we might develop an image of how they should be. Our first child is in fact a creature of this fantasy, and when they are born we may try to apply our imagined version to them. But if we hold on to the imagined child rather than the real one, and if he or she is unable to overwrite our fantasy, it does not bode well for their future – the child's life will become about nothing other than attaining our own needs, desires, and expectations.

*

The world-renowned psychoanalyst Alice Miller said that in many cases bringing up children is not about the children but about the adults. The whole process is determined according to the needs of the parents, who are convinced they know what is good for their children and push them in that direction.

Of course, it may sometimes be positive. In order not to dwell exclusively on the negative side of resolute parental ideas, let me mention an example from my own family. My paternal grandmother was desperate to study, but her parents didn't let her because of their own lack of education and because they didn't want her looking down on them. Her teacher asked them to allow bright little Rózsika to go to junior school, but her stepfather believed, 'All a girl needs to know is to take shelter when it rains.' My grandmother was so disappointed that she immediately made a pledge that if she had a child she would bring them up to aspire to earning a degree – in engineering, at that. She did not abandon her plan and devoted her whole life to my father's education. That was her great mission. In this case it was a godsend, for my father had a gift for everything technical, so the faculty of mechanical engineering was almost made for him. Even now, at the age of seventy-two, he is still driven by the desire to learn and acquire knowledge, and is always embarking on something new. We can guess at his latest enthusiasm from whatever specialist books are scattered throughout his apartment, be it beekeeping, sailing or computer-aided design. He had already imbibed the idea of lifelong learning in the cradle and, of course, he passed it on. I couldn't even tell you how many different courses I've been on!

Freedom of choice is a very important issue in your birth family: can you forge your own path and lead your own life, or must you follow your parents' ideas?

Questions:

- *Have you ever thought that you have to meet certain expectations, whether openly expressed or unspoken?*
- *How did the family formulate their expectations?*
- *Can you remember typical sentences in connection with your future? (For example, 'When you become a doctor/lawyer/soldier/actor . . .')*
- *Were you free to decide which sports to pursue, which musical instrument to play, or which school clubs to attend?*
- *Were you free to decide where to continue your studies?*
- *How was freedom of choice encouraged in your family?*

The replacement child

[. . .] to overcome the practical dragons that
stood in the way of the realization of my most
impossible fantasies.
Salvador Dalí, *The Secret Life of Salvador Dalí* [12]

The death of a child is an extremely difficult issue. In
the depth of our souls, we all have an idea about the
order of the world and we feel secure when events
follow that order. A child is the promise of the future;
our offspring (how expressive the word is, conjuring
a family tree where new members nestle beneath the
preceding generations) carry on the parents' lives. The
parents go ahead and the child follows them – both
in life and death. If this order is upset and a family
loses a child prematurely, it is extremely difficult to
live through – not only because an especially precious
thread of love is snapped, but our worldview is also
shattered. How can a child die whose task was to carry
on their parents' lives in themselves and with their own
children? How can one carry on living when one's most
fundamental convictions are lost by losing one's child?
The feeling of security and faith in a calculable and

predictable world ceases to exist along with a piece of the parental self.

Besides individual pain, such a grave trauma affects attachment between family members and influences the relationship between any surviving or subsequent child/ren and the parents. Researchers have identified three characteristic scripts. The silent guilty conscience is dominant in some families. They don't talk about the loss at all. The death of a sibling becomes a taboo. The unprocessed, suppressed feelings are latent as a heavy burden in the family system, and the living child is forced into a bitter role: they turn into the living memento of the loss. They not only fail to heal the wounds, but actually keep them open. There is no escape from this situation. Whenever the living child is seen, the lost child will come to mind, but since the family dares not acknowledge the pain, it is manifested as anger. The surviving child will be the target of that anger: they are criticised, maltreated, questioned and unloved. The child gradually comes to believe that they are bad, that everything is their fault, and assumes the family's guilty conscience, which will also have a catastrophic effect on their own future relationships.

A desperate man comes to see me. He has just divorced for the fourth time and asks me to find out why his relationships fail, one after another. It turns out that when he was three, his six-year-old brother was hit by a car. They were all leaving the house and were already standing in the street when the toddler began crying because he'd left his teddy bear inside. Their mother ran back into fetch it, which is when tragedy struck: his brother stepped out in front of a lorry and was killed instantly. His mother had a total breakdown, and her pain caused her almost to lose the power of speech. From then on, she hardly spoke to him, doing so only to criticise him or blame him for something. At the age of three, therefore, this man lost not only his brother, but also his mother. Love was replaced by rejection. What can a young child do to bear this? He tries for a while but then, if he does not succeed, steps back. He learns to distance himself from the source of both the pain and his own feelings. He avoids intimacy and suppresses his emotions.

So that's what he did. Instead of having feelings, he became a thinker. He studied and worked harder and harder, obsessively, to avoid idle moments. Whenever he met someone new, for a while he was on cloud nine – but within a few months, everything turned grey again. On these occasions he blamed the women for having tricked him, for making him believe that he could expect exciting, passionate love. After his fourth divorce, he began to think that perhaps he needed to examine his own role, in case it wasn't the women who were losing interest in the relationship but him. His childhood history sheds light on how deep an injury he carries; it prevents him from really committing himself.

His relationships start out fine, but when the thought of losing his partner becomes too painful, he swiftly withdraws his emotions. He experiences this withdrawal as his partner having become boring for him. It is a foolproof scheme that protects him from pain. In fact, all his life he has avoided the commitment that caused him so much suffering in childhood. Most startlingly, he realised that he didn't even dare establish a close relationship with his own children: he couldn't risk getting too attached to them, either, so he saw them just as 'friends'. In this way, his mother's withdrawal of love is now affecting her grandchildren.

On another occasion, a mother in mourning came to see me and told me her story.

> I was seven months pregnant when my two-year-old daughter died of leukaemia. I thought I would go mad with grief. When I gave birth, I couldn't even bring myself to look at the baby. I did not need that child, but the one who lay alone in the cemetery. I only wanted her back, no one else.

If a child can be lost and this causes such excruciating pain, the logic of the soul says that it would be better never to allow anyone else to become so dear to us. In this way, the surviving child is excluded and deprived of the chance of a relationship. The survivor's guilty conscience is bequeathed to them: 'If my sibling died,

I don't have a right to live either.' This conviction, of which the person is often unaware, may appear later on as a self-destructive life.

In other instances, the loss of a child makes parents so insecure that they overprotect the surviving or subsequent sibling. In practice, this involves constant and strict constraint, as well as excessive concern mixed with fear. 'Watch out, it's a dangerous world: tragedy may strike at any moment!' is what the parents express with their whole attitude. I have experienced this to my own cost. By the time my mother was born, my maternal grandmother had already lost two babies. My mother became her only child, and my grandmother could never love her freely and without anxiety. There was always something to protect her from. Later, when I was born, I too became the focus of my grandmother's fears. I was not allowed to go barefoot, as she was worried that I would catch a cold, develop an inflamed kidney, and die. In my grandmother's inner cinema, an ordinary household accident or childhood illness immediately projected the horror of death. 'Slippers!' I can still hear her shouting. And I can also hear myself nagging my own child in the same way. That's how we pass on the torch of fear from generation to generation.

The lives of Salvador Dalí and Vincent van Gogh come to mind when thinking of the third scenario of unresolved mourning. Apart from their both being world-renowned artists, we may think that they had little in common – yet their early years reveal something else.

Dalí was born just nine months after the death of his brother, also called Salvador, before the age of two, of a disease of the digestive system. Dalí's parents were convinced that their second son was the reincarnation of their deceased child and was born to replace him. When Dalí was five, they took him to his dead brother's grave, which had his own name on the stone. From then on Dalí thought of himself as the person who continued his dead brother's life. It does not seem too far-fetched to suggest that this must be connected with Dalí's search for an identity in young adulthood and his extreme way of living. In his autobiographical work *The Secret Life of Salvador Dalí*, he writes:

In my childhood I always did things 'differently from others,' but almost without being aware of it. Now, having finally understood the exceptional and phenomenal side of my pattern of behaviour, I 'did it on purpose.' It was only necessary for someone to say 'black' to make me counter 'white!' It was only necessary for someone to bow with respect to make me spit. My continual and ferocious need to feel myself 'different' made me weep with rage if some coincidence should bring me even fortuitously into the same category as others. Before all and at whatever cost: myself – myself alone! Myself alone! Myself alone!'[13]

These are shattering lines by a person who had learned early on never to be himself.

Vincent van Gogh was also named after his brother, who was stillborn a year to the day before his own birth (30 March 1852 and 1853). To make the situation even more bizarre, his birth was entered in the church register under the same number as that assigned to his deceased brother (number 29). Young Vincent was also frequently taken to his brother's grave in the cemetery. It is depressing to imagine what these visits meant to a developing personality. Yet the muddle did not end there. When the artist's beloved brother Theo had a son, he decided to name the baby Vincent Willem van Gogh. Although Theo had wanted to express his respect, van Gogh might equally have felt that his brother had replaced him with the infant, just as his parents had replaced his lost elder brother with him. Some have speculated that this could have been the final straw for the unstable artist who died by suicide half a year after the birth of his nephew.

Psychology refers to children born with the task of filling the immense void left by a deceased sibling as *replacement children*. The first study of the difficulties experienced by replacement children was published in 1964 by Albert and Barbara Cain. Their research and case studies show that if parental bereavement is halted, if parents deny their loss or try to move on too soon, it may deform the child's personality development in a pathological direction. The parents may unconsciously – or even openly, as seen in the two examples above – expect them to annul and cancel their sibling's death, to identify with them and carry on their curtailed life.

Being born to replace a deceased sibling in the parents' hearts can have a significant effect on how you lead your life, since with such expectations it is almost impossible to develop an independent identity. When the parents' desire is for us not to be ourselves but to become the person who passed away, the response is a pseudo-identity or false identity. Internal insecurity, uncertainty and impressionability appear when self-identity is lacking or absent. Replacement children automatically start off from a losing position, since death initiates processes of idealisation: the loss makes the deceased perfect. Thus the image of the lost child may become so embellished in the parents' souls that the younger sibling is unable to compete. Imagine that you constantly fell short of your 'angelic' sibling. Constantly experiencing failure can damage your self-respect, and you might adopt an incentiveless and passive-dependent approach to life. The feeling that 'I can never be good enough' grows in your personality, making it impossible to become a truly independent adult.

Who does not know the story of Peter Pan, the boy who refuses to grow up? What might not be so well known is that for its author, J. M. Barrie, writing the book was a way of processing his own trauma. Barrie was just six when his brother lost his life in an ice-skating accident the day before what would have been his fourteenth birthday.

Their mother broke down in pain. As she mourned, the young James sat by her bedside every night, trying to help her overcome her depression. To fulfil her wishes, he started to wear his brother's clothes and he even learned to whistle as his brother had done. When he turned fourteen, James mysteriously stopped growing. That was how he became the boy who wouldn't (or couldn't) grow up. Peter Pan's fantasy world is translated into Hungarian as *Nekeresdország* ('Don't Search Land') – but, as Kathleen Kelley-Lainé (a psychoanalyst of Hungarian heritage) notes, the original 'Neverland' far more tangibly expresses an unchanging realm where time does not pass, does not go forward, and is only repeated over and over again.

If you are born into a family where a child has already been lost (or if the tragedy happens during your life), it leaves an imprint on your soul for ever. You become a survivor and the psychic consequences of the loss are carried with you throughout life. The more trapped your parents are in their grief, the more difficult it is for them to let the dead child go and the more deformed their relationship with those who live on can become. The loss of a child reshapes the structure of a family: there will always be a missing member alongside the living.

When a child dies, there is a desire to banish suffering. This desire may awaken with overwhelming force. You might think that the birth of a new baby will help heal the pain. This is a natural inclination of the soul: to hurry forward, to overwrite and overcome the tragedy. People close to you often try to steer you in this direction, too. Barely a few months after losing her daughter, a client of mine was advised by her doctor – with good intentions, but knowing little about the nature of the soul – not to get fixated on the loss, saying she was still young and she should have another child as soon as possible. Mourning, however, demands its own time. If we deny it or cut it short too soon, we will pay the price.

A replacement child's life can turn out to be quite tragic, as if the soul were replaying the events of the original loss. Let me tell you a very sad story about this.

A woman dressed in black comes to my surgery. She is completely broken, exuding heart-rending sadness. She tells me that she lost her eighteen-year-old son in a car accident barely a month before. He had wanted a driving licence for his birthday and his parents agreed, albeit reluctantly as they were concerned for his safety. The son took driving lessons and could hardly wait to take his friends to a party on his eighteenth birthday. He passed the test with no mistakes. He was happy as a lark, so proud of himself, and so were his parents. The weather that day was fine. It became a bit overcast by the evening, but it seemed that the clouds were clearing and it wouldn't rain. The son set off from home, hooting the car's horn happily, while the parents waved from the gate, his mother calling to him to take care and drive carefully. Within twenty minutes, the sky had become dark and it began pouring with rain. Soon after, the parents heard ambulance sirens. An inner voice made them get straight in their car and drive as fast as they could along the route their son had taken. As they approached they could already see the car, which had swerved off the road and hit a tree. Paramedics were trying to resuscitate their son, fighting to save his life. After half an hour, they gave up. It is a tragic story. When you hear it, you are at a loss for words. The mother continued. She told me that nineteen years ago she had had another baby, also a boy, who had died unexpectedly at the age of three months. She thought the pain would drive her mad and that she could not survive the loss. Her family tried to comfort her and advised her not to pine away but rather to have another baby at once – which was what happened: she became pregnant that very month. Everybody regarded the new baby as a substitute for his brother; a child who could replace the irreplaceable. 'I did not want to mourn that one and now I must mourn two.' The sentence is uttered, full of remorse – and I know that there is a long road ahead before her pain will begin to subside.

Of course, not all children who are born after a dead sibling will become replacement children. If the parents are able to face bereavement, if they mourn appropriately and eventually let their lost child go, then the pain of unprocessed loss will not burden their relationship with the living siblings.

Recent research has also shown, however, that the role of a replacement child is not only prompted by the death of a sibling. This role is taken up whenever a child must meet certain expectations or fulfil specific desires originally required of another.

Let's consider, for example, the position of an adopted child. They most frequently arrive in a family because a long-expected biological baby never materialised. By then the parents are troubled by the accumulated frustrations and disappointments of years of unsuccessful attempts, but they have also envisaged what the child will be like once it's born. Adopted children arrive into this brightly coloured fantasy-space, and they are often expected, albeit unconsciously, to become identical to the child of the parents' imaginations. This unspoken pressure, which is precisely felt by the hidden registers of the psyche, complicates the evolution of the genuine self. If a child comes face to face with the request to 'be who I imagine you to be' instead of 'be who you are', they can do one of two things: they can either give up their own identity and try to fit in with the desired image, or they begin to spend their energy resisting and fighting against it. Two kinds of output, but neither bodes well for the evolution of the real self.

Of course, it must also be said that when the parents manage to understand and accept that their adopted child will always have two birthdays — one when they were born and another when they came to the new family — they can relate to one another in a beautiful way.

Imagine a family where one of the children is chronically ill. When you do so, you are probably primarily concerned with the position of the sick child, and for a long time, that was the attitude taken by researchers, too: only recently have they begun to study what happens to the *healthy* child, how *their* life is affected by the other's illness. Results indicate that illness reshapes the dynamics of a family to such an extent that it also exerts a strong influence over the healthy sibling's life.

Statistically, psychological disorders, such as depression, anxiety or OCD, are twice as likely to occur among children who grow up with a chronically ill sibling. These psychological disorders can even accompany them their whole lives, along with the feeling of having a guilty conscience, to become a basic experience for healthy siblings. They are constantly tormented and reproach themselves, 'Why am I healthy if my sibling is ill?'

I vividly remember, for example, a kind woman of about fifty whose life was overshadowed by remorse. Her younger brother was born with a serious genetic disease and given two to three years to live. The family pulled together and cared for him at home. The then five-year-old girl desperately tried to help her parents and constantly felt guilty for being fortunate enough to be able to run and play while her brother lay there helplessly. She chastised herself incessantly and over time became so adept at doing so that her guilty conscience was built into her self-image. If she had had to express in one sentence what kind of person she was, she would have

answered: 'I am guilty.' Even in adulthood, this tormenting feeling became a barrier, blocking her ability to form
intimate relationships.

If one of their children requires increased care, parents may develop two characteristic attitudes, usually
unintentionally. One is that the care for and medical
treatment of the sick child consumes all their attention,
strength, and physical and emotional capacity, and as a
result the requirements of the healthy child are put on
the back burner. 'Wait a minute, you know I have to look
after your sick sister!'; 'You're so clever, you can see that
she needs more attention now!'; 'Listen to me: go and
play, don't you bother me too!' To spare the parents, the
healthy sibling becomes a tiptoeing shadow. They feel
redundant. The film *Wonder* (2017) presents such a family.
My heart sinks at some scenes – for example, when the
healthy little girl says:

> I've never asked my mom for help with my homework.
> I've never needed my dad to remind me to study for a
> test. I just did most of my studying in waiting rooms
> and hospitals. Mom and Dad would always say I was
> the most understanding girl in the world. I don't know
> about that. I just knew my family couldn't take one
> more thing.

But the other approach doesn't hold much promise
for the healthy child either. In this scenario the child
is the centre of attention as the parents' 'only hope'.

All possible expectations fall on this child, who has to accomplish twice as much in order to reduce her parents' frustrations and fears.

It must be noted that the above scripts are not set in stone. How a family functions when caring for a permanently sick child and the effect this has on the healthy sibling depend on several factors. If the family has access to satisfactory resources, either external or internal, they can significantly moderate the negative effects.

Questions:

- *Have you felt that your family's behaviour was strange or incomprehensible to you?*
- *Did your family have a child who was lost before your birth?*
- *Did you have a sibling who was lost during your life?*
- *In the cases of death, to what extent could the family talk about it openly, or was the topic taboo?*
- *Could you ask questions about what had happened, and did you get satisfactory answers?*
- *In your opinion, to what degree did your family manage to process the loss of the child/children? (Don't forget to include instances that happened in previous generations.)*
- *Were you ever compared to your deceased sibling or to a child lost in earlier generations?*
- *Do or did you have a permanently sick sibling?*

— *What expressed or unspoken expectations did you have*
 to meet in connection with that?
— *Did your family tell you that you were their only hope?*
— *Did you ever get the feeling that you were more sheltered*
 than was reasonable?
— *Have you felt an incomprehensible guilty conscience?*
— *Was there a permanently sick person among your*
 predecessors? How do you feel it influenced the social
 network of your family?

Birth order

You don't live in a world all alone. Your
brothers are here, too.
Albert Schweitzer[14]

It can be impossible to comprehend how two brothers could lead radically different lives. While one falters from one failure to another or is trapped in cycles of addiction, the other has a balanced life with no major problems, a fulfilling family life and a good career. How is this possible when they were both brought up in the same family? The short answer is that no two children grow up in the same family – at least in a psychological sense. As many children as there are in a family, so there are as many different emotional situations to be born into, each with a different innate temperament. Each child in a family has a very different experience and lives their own unique life.

Alfred Adler, Freud's first follower and later his first disloyal disciple, examined how birth order shaped one's course of life. He was convinced that a person's place in the family affected their character. Various research groups verify this thesis one day only to refute it a year later. How the constellation of siblings affects our fate is certainly a question that continues to occupy professionals. Often our relationships with our siblings are the longest we have in life, and so their effect – be it positive or negative – cannot be easily ignored when we ponder how we've become who we are.

In *The Birth Order Book*,[15] American psychologist Kevin Leman asks us to consider several other important factors related to this issue. Let's see what they are.

Age difference. In the case of an age difference of more than six years, it is not really possible to speak of a brotherly or sisterly relationship in the traditional sense. In this situation, both children are characterised by the features of an only child – by the time the younger child is ready for intensive interaction, the older one is already busy with their peer group or has already left the family.

An age difference of two to three years is traditionally regarded as ideal because by then the elder sibling is increasingly interested in the outside world and, in the case of a firm emotional relationship, no longer requires the mother's constant physical closeness. The birth of a younger sibling may of course make the elder temporarily more attached again, perhaps longing for more attention, cuddles, and care.

Gender. While in the USA and Western Europe there is an increasing focus on gender-neutral treatment, in Hungary I continue to observe parents strongly emphasising gender differences, both in their emotional attitude and communication. Recently while shopping I witnessed a mother turning to her crying two-year-old son saying: 'Boys don't cry: it's girls who get emotional.' I would have liked to ask her how many times her husband's repressed emotions had upset her, or how often she'd been shocked when a man referred to her sorrow or pain as hysterics. If it happened even once, it would be worth considering whether this foolish practice of socialisation was healthy.

However, the fact remains that parents still treat children of different genders differently. They traditionally forbid boys to manifest pain, fear and sorrow, regarding it as a sign of weakness, while they disapprove of girls expressing anger and behaving in an assertive manner.

The parents' own birth-order position. What are parents, after all, but former children, who carry their earliest experiences over into their parental roles? For example, the firstborn, who are most often more conservative and compliant, might manage their family more strictly, or they might compensate for their own former negative experiences of excessively high expectations by treating their own firstborn more complaisantly and permissively. Another interesting observation is that parents usually find it easiest to relate to the child with whom they share the same birth order.

Patchwork, blended, or step-families. How telling it is that there are so many different terms for when a third system is formed from two families following divorce or the death of a parent — as if indicating what a particularly complex emotional situation this can be, and one that is often so difficult to perceive clearly and, especially, to treat. In this case, the child may occupy different positions in the new family established by the father or the mother, which of course presents an extra stimulus. When a fight broke out at home between siblings of different 'litters', the great Hungarian writer Frigyes Karinthy (1887–1938) is said to have remarked to his second wife, the psychiatrist Aranka Böhm (1893–1944), 'Aranka, please: your child and my child are fighting with our child!'

Dissimilar parental treatment. 'We love each of our children in the same way,' parents insist – yet when the siblings themselves are asked, they can say precisely which parent/grandparent favours which child and who gets special treatment from whom. It is a social requirement – and also a mother's and father's personal wish – to treat each child equally, but in most cases the emotional quality of their relationships will be different, totally involuntarily (sometimes causing lifelong damage). One client of mine relates how their parents used to treat their siblings differently. 'My elder brother never had to get up early on Sundays. If I'd dared stay in bed beyond 7 a.m., I would have been dealt with!' 'After the remark "Someone should vacuum the room", my mother always pointed at me. In this case I was always "someone" while my elder sister was a nobody. I would have liked to be a nobody – for once at least!'

One might think that the favoured child would do better, but experience proves otherwise. Parental treatment can have a profound effect on every child's personality development. Peter, a man in his late thirties, still remembers with deep remorse that he didn't protect his younger brother from their father's abuse. While the father never raised his hand to Peter, he regularly hit and insulted Peter's brother, who was two years younger. Even today, Peter harbours ambivalent sentiments towards people who symbolise power: he fears them, but at the same time tries to do his best to please them. He has lost all contact with his younger brother: they haven't talked to each other for years.

Different treatment is very powerful in forming the course of your life, since everything you experience in your early years, the way you are treated and responded to, gets built into your personality.

Firstborn children can be said to initiate their parents in the parental way of life. It is they with whom every-thing happens first: the excitement of pregnancy, the first nappy change, teething . . . the list goes on. For some time, their position is privileged as all attention is directed their way, and they are most often overpro-tected. As adults, firstborn children often function with conservative composure. They will be leaders rather than avant-garde innovators. They are more likely to safeguard traditions and maintain their parents' values. For centuries, the privileged position of the firstborn was clear: firstborn males were the sole inheritors of the family's estate and enjoyed priority in education, too. While his teacher did his best to convince my great-grandfather that my paternal grandfather (born second) should be sent to university instead of his less talented and less motivated elder brother, my great-grandfather was unyielding. Tradition is tradition: the older one studies while the younger one 'toils'.

International research shows that firstborn children are still more highly qualified, with more occupying leading positions and earning more than younger siblings. The nineteenth-century polymath Francis Galton stated that firstborn children were in the majority among prominent scientists and were over-represented among Nobel Prize winners; more than half of American presidents were born first in their families.

According to evolutionary psychologists, our modern skulls contain Stone Age brains, and all human behaviour and characteristics have survived by having at some point offered a selective advantage. They think that it is no accident that those who are firstborn enjoy privileges in the family. If the primary aim of human behaviour is the maintenance of the species, then it is absolutely understandable. According to this theory, parents have an innate, natural calculator that helps to decide what quantity and quality of parental involvement is required for their genes to be passed on to the next generation. According to the theory of parental involvement, the older child is generally less volatile than the younger sibling, because by the time the younger one enters the world as a weak newborn, the older one has already given some proof of their ability to survive, therefore it is 'more worth' investing in their life and securing the larger part of the resources for them – in other words, treating them with an advantage.

Interestingly, being the firstborn involves a different neurobiological function. Surveys of monkeys have shown that when firstborn infants were taken to an alien environment, their stress responses increased more sharply than those of their younger siblings – as if nature had designed firstborns more carefully, so that they would not needlessly go looking for trouble. After all, who knows whether there will be another chance for future descendants?

There are two sides to the coin; being the firstborn is a considerably ambivalent experience. On the positive side, there is the parents' time, access and resources. On the other side, there is their inexperience, anxiety, inhibitions and all the expectations that can be set for a child. An old anecdote says that if we drop the firstborn's dummy on the floor, we sterilise it; with the second child we hold it briefly under running water; with the third we blow off the dust – and with the fourth child's dummy we're happy if the dog fetches it and puts it back in the child's mouth. My younger brother and his wife have three children, so I have had the opportunity to experience this change first-hand. With their firstborn they weighed the baby before each feed, noted down the result, then fed the child, followed by further weighing and note-taking. This was so that they could see after each feed whether the baby had had the necessary amount. It didn't matter that this bouncing baby was positively bursting with health, my brother and his wife were still so unsure that they trusted the scales more than their own eyes. By the time their third child was born, they did not have the time to be unsure!

In the absence of a sibling, firstborns become only children. Even the phrase 'only child' sounds a bit depreciative, and these children have often been regarded as selfish and less adaptive, spoilt little eager beavers who were unable to function in a team. Indeed, this mistaken attitude spread to such an extent that some companies were purportedly reluctant to hire candidates who had grown up as only children. (The question of sibling position first manifests itself within the family, and later arises again at a societal level.)

Only children must meet all their parents' (often contradictory) expectations on their own. For example, I have an acquaintance whose mother at times wanted her to be an outstanding actor and at other times an excellent doctor. These ambivalent wishes resulted in her dropping out from three universities – and she still has a dilemma about what she really wants to be. One could say that she should be herself, but her problem is that she hasn't got a clue who she really is.

A woman about to turn forty comes to me because she has never had a relationship and this situation is becoming increasingly difficult for her. Her mother, who lives in the country, is personally offended that she cannot find a partner. Whenever they talk, the dreadful question is posed: 'And have you met anyone yet?' Of course, she wants to comply and arranges dates as if they were on an assembly line, but nothing serious comes from them. She is such a pretty, intelligent and friendly woman, I can hardly imagine that no men have taken a liking to her. What can the matter be? I ask myself, and soon find the answer. Since the devil is always in the detail, I ask my clients to be as precise as possible about their everyday lives: how do they live, what do they do throughout the day, what do they do at the weekends? I do this in the case of this woman, too, and among other things she tells me – and at this my ears prick up – that she goes home to her parents at least once a fortnight. She likes being with them and her mother explicitly requires her to be 'at home'. She refers to her parents' house as 'home', although she has had her own home for years, and spends quite a lot of time with her parents. I ask her how her life would change if she had a partner. At first, she looks at me as if she doesn't understand the question, but then she says she wouldn't want anything to change.

'All right, let's see exactly what would happen. Let's imagine it as a film.' At first she goes with her partner to see her parents every other weekend; later, when they have children, they all make the pilgrimage together. 'Come rain or snow, even if the child is ill, or if her husband once in a blue moon wants to do something else – always.' As we think it over, she covers her face with her hands anxiously and asks: 'Oh, my gosh, how will I manage that?' 'There's no way,' I answer and at the bottom of her heart she seems to know exactly what I mean. She doesn't really give men a chance. She is simply not ready for the change that goes with having a relationship and a family of one's own. This young woman is writhing in the trap of her parents' contradictory expectations: at one and the same time, she has to marry and 'present grandchildren' to her parents, while remaining an eternal child who regularly runs home to the family nest where her arrival is the highlight of an otherwise dull everyday life. Moreover, deep down she realises that as an only child she will have to arrange for her parents' care in their old age. We agree that this is a very real problem that in all probability she herself will have to resolve. However, that's a question for another day, since her parents are still youthful and fit as a fiddle, and right now she should not put her life on the back burner.

The question of siblings – or their absence – can shape our lives in such subtle and elaborate ways. The arrival of a sibling removes the firstborn from the throne of exclusivity. The firstborn is the one for whom the sibling's birth is the most unexpected (for those who are born later, the presence of another child is a basic experience). Even if the firstborn longed for the secondborn, they were certainly unprepared for most changes. I hardly know any families where the firstborn did not suddenly realise 'I wasn't banking on that!' and didn't propose that the sibling be 'removed' as soon as possible. 'He's been here long enough now: let's take him back to the hospital!' says the child to his parents; or, when visitors are saying goodbye, the child suggests that they could take the baby away with them, reassuring them that the family will do just fine without him or her. As for me, on my own initiative I tried to get rid of my newborn baby brother, by filling his mouth with a chocolate bar when he was just a few days old. My stunt, of course, was not an astounding success, which confirmed for me beyond any doubt that I was lumbered with a horrid intruder.

If we return to the evolutionary theory, nothing is more understandable than sibling rivalry. The so-far exclusively held resources (in this case the parents' attention, love and care) are, from a certain point on, accessible to only a limited extent. And make no mistake, you have to fight because what's at stake is nothing less than life itself – thus says the Stone Age mind. The firstborn follows this natural law, openly, if possible; if not, then the storm of protest swells within. (Yes, I am aware of exceptions, but here we are talking about typical behaviour.)

In cases where a child experiences prolonged feelings of exclusion, this may become a relationship pattern. (And here it does not matter whether the parents tried to ease the firstborn's feelings or ignored them completely, because children respond not to factual events but to the parents' internal image and to subjective reality, as they experience it.) A number of my firstborn clients struggle with an internal dilemma about whether they are valuable enough, good enough, whether they are truly wanted and loved. During our sessions, painful childhood stories keep coming up in which, as they remember them, the younger sibling received more attention and care than they did. A young woman, for example, has recently found out that family videos not only recorded Christmases and birthdays, but also captured her desperate attempts to be listened to. In these recordings her voice can be heard shouting that the family should look how high she climbed the ladder or how deftly she dribbled the ball, the camera only eventually being pointed in her direction several minutes later. 'I wasn't the important one,' she tells herself today, slowly realising that she constantly recreates this familiar situation in her relationships. Despite her best intentions, she starts relationships with non-committal men and has to settle for mere scraps of attention and a stop–start pattern of presence and care.

The *secondborn* arrives in a ready-made family system. Parents do a lot with more experience, yet it also means that rules and customs are already present. The secondborn's task is to push the boundaries and shape the family system according to their own requirements. Secondborn are often avant-garde or rebellious, and sometimes have radical approaches. Indeed, this is usually true not only of secondborns, but also of subsequent children. If you look at the people who launch revolutions, it's interesting that there are eighteen times more later-born children than firstborns. Scientists who introduce the world to radically new concepts are also more likely to be non-firstborns: for example, Copernicus (who in 1510 was the first to suggest that it is the Earth that orbits the Sun, a notion regarded as heretical at the time) was the youngest of five siblings; and Charles Darwin, the father of evolutionary theory, which was also considered shocking in its time, was the fifth of six children.

The younger child observes their elder sibling, who is the most obvious role model: they imitate them, following them everywhere and trying to participate in their activities. The younger child is also, often, jealous of the elder. A still hurt thirty-year-old secondborn once said to me: 'There were enough photos taken of my elder sister to fill three albums – whereas there are only four photos of me.' The second child (and of course any that follow) gets less time devoted to them: after all, the elder child is always somewhere nearby. This causes quite a bit of guilt for the parents, which they try to compensate for in some way, most often with extra concessions.

An interesting observation is that the secondborn more often become *index patients*, that is children who draw attention to themselves with something negative, whose troubles and problematic behaviour require intervention from outside the family. According to Adler, the secondborn will be a rebel who tries to overthrow the elder sibling's power. And black sheep are more often represented among the secondborn – let's not forget that the biblical prodigal son was a second in the birth order. The situation can become especially dangerous if the family unit is full of conflicts and the younger sibling is identified as a scapegoat on whom all other family members can vent their spleen.

Secondborn children often seek contacts outside the family. They have more friends and fit into a community of people with ease. I remember how much I envied my younger brother who recruited a group of friends for himself with no bother at all, while I was anxious to behave properly so that our parents could be proud of me.

If there is a relatively large age difference between the first- and secondborn, the elder often adopts a parental role, meaning that there are effectively three people in charge of the younger sibling. This is called a *parentified situation*, and it is thought to leave a mark on our whole life and on our choice of partners. (I'll write about parentification in more detail in Part Four.) If a third sibling is born, the secondborn becomes a 'sandwich child', who gets squeezed in the often rather narrow space between the eldest and youngest children. Such a child can in fact feel that there is hardly any time left for them amidst the family chaos. 'My big brother is the eldest, my little brother is the baby, but who am I?' asked a middle boy, with some justification, when his brother was born. This insecure search for identity and the feeling of being disregarded may accompany the middle child even in adulthood.

Kevin Leman, author of the aforementioned *Birth Order Book*, recalls a funny story. When his book was published in the United States, he received several reproachful letters from middle children. One wrote:

Dear Dr Leman,

I noticed that in your Birth Order Book you devoted fewer pages to middle children than to any other member of the birth order. I know for sure because I counted them. Why so? A neglected middle [. . .]

Dr Leman's answer was: 'So what? Big deal! Haven't you got used to it yet?' Later, he admitted that his humorous comment masked a significant amount of professional uncertainty, which was the real reason why he wrote less about middle children: they pose the hardest problems for researchers. However, what can be said about them, in general, is that they have the ability to compromise, and a bent for independent thinking, as well as a skill for diplomacy.

The birth of a third child is accompanied by an important new possibility that cannot be neglected: exclusion. Human beings are meant to form partnerships, and so when there are three siblings it is almost inevitable that one of the children will be left out. This was so natural for a young client of mine that she did not even notice it. When she talked about her childhood, she never mentioned any kind of conflict. However, it seemed to me that something was not right. She had been seeing me for some time because it bothered her that she'd got into a series of relationships with unavailable men. Her partners were usually married and didn't have the slightest intention of divorcing their wives. For a while our analyses produced little by way of results and we were unable to get close to the reasons. (On these occasions one senses the lengths to which the psyche goes to hide its oppressive contents from ourselves.) Nevertheless, it suddenly struck me at one point that her whole family (her parents, the grown-up children, and grandchildren) travelled from time to time, but that this woman always went somewhere else. When the family went skiing, she was on the beach; if the family went to stay at a spa hotel, she set off in the opposite direction to tour Transylvania. On the third such occasion I asked her what on earth was going on. That question started deeper work until at last we could talk about the lifelong feeling of childhood exclusion. To her astonishment she realised that what had been a familiar experience for years was now happening in her love affairs: to remain outside of a union, observing with longing how good it is for the happy couple, and then trying in vain to worm her way between them. The aim, therefore, was not to find a married man who was prepared to get a divorce, but to form an internal conviction that she deserved a place in a relationship and to reject the role of the spare. Of course, internal, unconscious beliefs cannot be transformed from one day to another. Our earliest experiences permanently imprint the possible scripts of our lives. If someone often experienced exclusion in their childhood it is difficult for them to believe that they may have a place in the inner circle, that they can be wanted, accepted and included. In such cases, therapy is nothing less than a viscerally affecting experience of acceptance. From week to week, clients begin to experience the feeling of being expected, the knowledge that there is somewhere where they have a place, and someone who accepts them openly and without judgement. Sadly, for many people a therapist is the first person who makes them feel valued but, as a result of repeated sessions, they are slowly able to transform their deep-set beliefs. This was the case for my client: a woman who used to play minor roles in her relationships is now happily married.

The little one. To be the youngest in the family has many advantages. By the time the last child arrives, their parents are 'true pros' and easily perform the routine tasks which had caused them anxiety with their first child. The family has grown to a size and there simply isn't enough time, attention or capacity to keep to the same rules and routines as before and, consequently, youngest children grow up with more freedom. The result of this more relaxed upbringing can be frequently observed in the roles they take on. Youngest children mostly want to excel and draw attention to themselves by clowning about and making fun. In some families, the youngest child may be favoured by the parents – they are the 'little sweetie'. It is with the youngest child that parents can experience for the final time the joy of having a baby. Mothers are aware of this and usually say that this child is their last chance to enjoy this intensive early relationship. However, if the parents for some reason get stuck in this approach and can relate to the youngest child only as their 'little baby', this may hinder the child's development.

A mother came to see me at one point because her youngest (eight-year-old) child refused to use the toilet and still wore a nappy. They had sought help wherever they could, the child was examined through and through, but no physical explanation had been found. Psychologists recommended various behavioural-therapy tricks, yet they only achieved pseudo-results: after two days, the child again demanded the nappy. I asked the mother to talk to me about her family, which she did with a glint in her eye. Then I prompted her to tell me to what extent this family was different from what she had wanted. It turned out that she came from a large family and she herself had wanted at least five children, but her husband drew a line at three. He told her, 'That's it, no more children! Mother this one all you like – but then we're done with babies!' The woman accepted her husband's advice and by keeping her youngest in nappies she unconsciously kept her well-developed, healthy child in the position of a baby as long as she could.

Nappying not only presented a way of holding on to the intimate relationship between the mother and her baby, it also meant preserving a life situation that would not be open to her in the future: parenting young children. Just two sessions were needed before the child was out of nappies and using the toilet in the most natural manner. Before anybody thinks that I have some extraordinary skills, I'd like to set your mind at rest. All I did was follow the basic principle of child therapy, which is always to look beyond the child's symptoms to the parents. Children are symptom carriers, and if they have problems, it is best to analyse the parents thoroughly and resolve their own struggles. This mother felt that her life would not be complete unless she had at least five children, and though she could not resist her husband's desire for a smaller family when he clearly drew the line at three children, neither could she fully accept his decision – she was mourning her lost, desired vision of the future. Therapy gave her the opportunity to express her pain while talking about how afraid she was of letting her ideal family go, and in doing so her tension was released. Her child unconsciously detected that release and was finally able to behave according to her age.

Twins. If anyone has experienced symbiosis, the constant presence of the other, twins have. Twins begin to share their experience as embryos: ultrasound images show how intensively they can communicate with each other;

and nearly everyone has seen photos on social media of newborn twins holding each other's hands or embracing one another.

Twins always receive special attention. Their whole situation is interesting because it is unusual. Wherever they go, they are observed with curiosity and asked dozens of questions – particularly if they are identical. This extra attention doesn't leave personality development unaffected: twins can easily form a sense that they are special, which accompanies them throughout their life.

The private world of twins is manifested in the characteristic features of their speech development. A specific language, a so-called 'autonomous speech' only they understand, develops in at least 40 per cent of twin relationships. Since twins understand each other perfectly, they don't have to learn to express their thoughts in words understandable to the outside world and as a result they often begin to speak 'properly' later than non-twins.

The problem of developing an independent identity is a problematic by-product of being identical twins. Just think how difficult it is to be ourselves when the other is always hanging on to us, someone who looks exactly like us, has the same toys and, what's more, is dressed in the same clothes. (By now the movement of 'dressing twins alike' is fortunately dwindling.) If twins are not helped in their early years to discover their own unique personality, they may be stuck in a system of a mutually dependent relationship, perhaps for the rest of their lives.

I've recently seen a sad example of this involving two young women. The elder sister (although she was born only a few minutes earlier) had always taken care of her younger sister. Their surroundings reinforced it. 'How well you're looking after Klára!' This mollycoddling was so pleasant that in the end Klára didn't want to give it up, even as an adult. While her elder sister graduated from university, got married and had two children, Klára just drifted through life, idling along, and all the while pining for her sister's pampering. She follows her sister everywhere like a shadow and has been unable to lead her own life. Even today she 'practically lives' at her sister's. She has her own room and privileges, and has a fierce rivalry with her nieces, who can hardly approach their own mother. The whole family, and now the subsequent generation, suffer from Klára's inability to separate.

As the above example shows, the effect of birth order is not necessarily set in stone. The various theories outlined here serve rather as a starting point for considering what has influenced one's own circumstances. As parents, the theories may help us attend to participating in our children's lives as consciously as possible.

Questions:

- *Do you have a brother or sister?*
- *Do you have unborn siblings (because of abortion or miscarriage), or did the family lose a child after you were born?*

- *Where do you come in the birth order?*
- *What was your relationship with your sibling/s?*
- *Has your relationship with your sibling/s changed over the years? In what way?*
- *Which parent did you feel was closer to you?*
- *Which sibling was the favourite of which parent or grandparent?*
- *How was this manifested?*

PART TWO
Trauma

The affections of soul are inseparable from the
material substratum of animal life, to which we
have seen that such affections, e.g. passion and
fear, attach, and have not the same mode of
being as a line or a plane.

Aristotle, *De Anima* (*On the Soul*)[1]

The earthquake of the psyche

> If we conspire to erase the past from our
> memories and shield our children's minds
> from the horrors of those years, we will be
> failing in our duty to the future.
> Ludmila Ulitskaya, *Daniel Stein, Interpreter*[2]

When we encounter shocking events, instead of facing what happened our strong inclination is to look away or to downplay the incidents, or we might even decide that the victim's own provocative behaviour was the cause of the trouble. Why do we do this? Why do we try to deny images of pain and, by some manoeuvre, exclude them from our mind? When calamity strikes someone, why do we find it so easy to say 'they got what they deserved'? How can we look aside when we see suffering?

Social psychologist Melvin Lerner suggests that we all have a notion that the world is morally fair. In psychology this concept is referred to as *a belief in a just world*, or the just-world fallacy. According to Lerner, the belief that good is ultimately rewarded and evil punished is key to preserving our psychological wellbeing.

It is a cognitive distortion that helps maintain the feeling of predictability, security and control, since if we lose our belief in a world where monstrosities only happen with reason it can bring about dangerous consequences: we may lose our motivation and feel that our lives are meaningless and all our efforts futile. Therefore we choose to maintain the illusion, even when it is clearly not true.

And this is not true just of individuals: entire societies would rather bury their heads in the sand when they find themselves facing life's grim realities. This attitude, which could be said to have been the norm for decades, prevented us from investigating how the experience of suffering carried within affects our future lives, and also the lives of our children.

As Judith Herman notes in her book *Trauma and Recovery*,[3] the modern world's first mass experience of suffering, fear and threat came with the First World War. (Let's not distance ourselves too much: this was the era of our grandparents and great-grandparents.) When war broke out at the end of July 1914, men set off to the front with pride: contemporary films show soldiers waving cheerfully, little suspecting what awaited them. The German emperor Wilhelm II encouraged his troops by saying they would be back home 'before the leaves fall from the trees'. His promise proved to be unduly optimistic, since the leaves had fallen four more times by the time the Great War ended, and soldiers were able to return from the front, having endured horrors that, until then, would have been unthinkable. Modern military techniques made killing tragically efficient. The world had never witnessed such levels of human destruction. The troops confined to the trenches had no chance of escape, they just waited helplessly for the terrifying end. This was an ordeal for which neither they nor the high command had been prepared, not to mention the incomprehension of everyone else. As the months went by, the number of soldiers who went to pieces psychologically presented a grave problem for the army. The men who fought on the front displayed symptoms that had previously been thought of as characteristic of neurotic women: they cried, sobbed, screamed frantically or sat rigidly, staring into nothingness. Their situation was made even more difficult because in public opinion and among physicians there was a presumption that the main problem was a personality flaw. At the time, the existence of psychic trauma was flatly rejected. The public thought that real men and especially real patriotic men should not cry or break down even with bombs exploding nearby, torn bodies lying around them, and fellow soldiers dying in their arms. The tormented soldiers returning from war were left entirely on their own with their nightmares and harrowing and haunting memories. During the war they had been trapped in the trenches, but in its aftermath, it was their rejection by their environment that locked them up in a silent prison. Today we know that people bury their pain very deeply indeed when they do not have the opportunity to talk about horrors they have experienced, or if those around them turn a deaf ear or, even, put the blame on them.

By the time of the Second World War, it was more or less recognised that however strong a character or stable a personality someone was, they were likely to break down after about two hundred days on the front. This isn't about human failings; psychic trauma is nothing other than an entirely natural reaction of the nervous system when facing threats, death and violence. However, the long-lasting consequences were still to be reckoned with. Yet another war was needed for the topic of trauma to come into prominence. Soldiers returning from Vietnam were the first to resist pressure to be silenced and to make the public aware of the devastating effects of war. Research began that proved beyond doubt that the monstrosities soldiers experienced at the front had an effect on their later lives and, moreover, on the lives of their children and families. Psychological trauma cannot be forgotten, wiped out or invalidated.

The transgenerational transmission of traumas was first pinpointed by the seemingly inexplicable psychological condition of the children of Holocaust survivors. People who often knew nothing of their parents' sufferings nevertheless carried the distant imprints of the horror in mysterious ways — in the form of anxiety disorders, depression and apparently unjustified fears and phobias. New research accumulated, increasing proof that the past lived on viscerally in the descendants.

In 1980, post-traumatic stress disorder (PTSD) was included in the classification scheme of mental disorders in DSM-III, the third edition of the American Psychiatric Association's *Diagnostic and Statistical Manual of Mental Disorders*.* It was finally officially acknowledged that the effects of painful events in life can be retained in the long term, and today the transgenerational transmission of trauma has become a leading field of research.

These days the word *trauma* is often used for tiny difficulties or unpleasant situations, and as a result the term has become almost meaningless. People call all sorts of stressful situations 'traumatic' when they are often nothing of the sort. Although all trauma involves a situation of stress, not all stressful situations are traumatic or traumatising. But where is the boundary between a difficulty in life and a trauma? How can the essence of trauma be grasped more precisely?

Difficulties, trials and crises naturally accompany our lives. We stumble along, face painful situations, become disappointed in ourselves and in others, and suffer losses – these are unavoidable elements of what we call life. However, when we talk about a trauma, we must consider an experience with a far deeper effect.

When we face a threat, the sympathetic nervous

---

* A guide to symptoms whereby someone can be diagnosed with various kinds of mental disorder.

system, in a state of excitement, mobilises our whole organism. Ancient mechanisms switch on in a moment: all our organs and tiny cells are activated, each in their own way, to ensure our survival. Adrenaline levels rise, blood pressure increases, our heart thumps vehemently, our breathing becomes rapid, muscles tense, pupils enlarge, while the function of the stomach and intestines slows down. The struggle against threat and danger generally assumes two forms, with the situation determining which provides the better chance of survival: *fight* or *flight*. But what happens if there is no opportunity for either? If we are compelled to bear what's happening to us helplessly, defencelessly and powerlessly? In such circumstances – at moments of terror when the hitherto familiar and comprehensible world falls to pieces – traumatic reactions develop. No wonder we draw parallels between trauma and the devastation of an earthquake. A trauma is the earthquake of the psyche. Imagine that a natural catastrophe like those we see on TV takes place in our own internal world. Everything that had been familiar is suddenly upturned and lost. When we are under threat, our earlier concept of the world, the knowledge we thought certain, crumbles to nothingness. The framework that, until then, made life manageable, predictable and foreseeable falls apart. Earlier contingency plans and ways of approach are worth nothing in these situations. Traumatic events imbue those who experience them with a paralysing fear. They lose control over what happens. Their view of the world and also their self-image is shattered. 'Who am I that this can happen to me? How can I regard myself after this?'

Those who experience a grave trauma lose something very important: their sense of security. From then on, they are always on alert because they feel that they never know what's going to happen at any moment. Their world is now tinged with darkness. They have to keep their eyes peeled and watch out for possible attacks. This is not merely a temporary state – the truth of trauma is that something that has ended is not truly over: peace is declared after a war, concentration-camp prisoners are liberated, victims are removed from abusive families, but the dread and fear live on.

This is what became identified as PTSD. One very characteristic symptom of this extremely complex disorder is that survivors of trauma are tortured by flashbacks. Much as they would like to forget, painful images keep reappearing in their mind's eye as if the past were becoming real again. Not only do they see what happened, they experience the suffering in their body and in each of its cells. Even tiny details that recall the traumatic situation (for example, a particular scent, or the way the light falls on an object) are sufficient for the affected person to find themselves once again right in the middle of the horror.

A Vietnam veteran's wife talked about how it felt to experience this at close hand. Long after the war, she and her husband took their children to a funfair.

Everyone was waiting excitedly to go on the main attraction, a huge swing that moved up and down, left and
right. While the children and other adults laughed and
screamed happily, her husband's face turned white as a
sheet. Through pursed lips all he said was that if the ride
were not stopped at once, he would jump. Many years
after the war, that otherwise jolly situation reminded him
of the dreadful moments he had experienced as a young
helicopter pilot attacking the jungle, flying up and down,
left and right.

When we experience a traumatic situation, our self-
defence system switches on, and it does not switch off
even after the danger ends. It's as if our body told us to
watch out because the horror might strike again at any
time. This condition, in which our vegetative or autonomous nervous system gets stuck in a state of chronic alert,
is called *hyperarousal*. Usually we are not conscious of it,
yet we feel somehow tense and restless and can't easily
fall asleep, or we wake up with a start and toss and turn
sleeplessly.

In several of his books and lectures, Bessel van der Kolk,
a leading trauma researcher, explains that when we are
under extreme threat, something peculiar happens to our
nervous system. Our thinking falls apart and becomes
disjointed; pieces of information bypass the higher cerebral areas and penetrate very deeply to the non-verbal
unconscious levels, where they are imprinted as physical
sensations, fragmented images, emotions, and snippets

of recollection. This is why it is so difficult, and often impossible, to talk about our most painful memories. While many victims endure suffering helplessly, they disassociate from the events (in other words they enter an altered state of consciousness) in order to cope with the horror. For example, a client of mine was able to endure his father hitting him with a metal belt buckle by imagining he was in a shiny bubble nibbling some cake with soft music playing. Even today, nearly forty years after the events, he cannot wear a belt because the mere sight of one causes him palpitations.

At the same time, traumatic memories keep appearing not only in flashbacks or in regularly recurring nightmares but also in acts. Freud called this *repetition compulsion* and thought that in such repetitions the psyche tried to rewrite what had happened with the possibility of finding a less terrible script. Abused children might not consciously remember the awful incidents of their past, but those events can reappear in their stubbornly repeated games. This type of re-enactment may be behind the phenomenon where generations in a family keep repeating unprocessed traumas.

The psychotherapist Alessandra Cavalli once gave a presentation in Hungary about the transgenerational transmission of trauma in which she outlined an interesting case from her own practice. The parents had contacted her because for months their anorexic adolescent daughter had been willing to eat no more than a few bites of bread each day. She was wasting away to skin and bone, and the family began to fear that they were going to lose her. By the time they saw the therapist, the situation had in fact become critical. As an expert in the transgenerational transmission of trauma, Cavalli suspected that it wasn't only the girl's life she would have to dig into. She was not mistaken. At a meeting with the whole of the girl's family, her quietly spoken grandmother suddenly started to talk. It turned out that she had been born in Germany and was deported during the Second World War. It was a kind of miracle that she survived the concentration camp, albeit as a skeletal human wreck. She never saw her parents and siblings again: they all met their deaths in the camp. Like many of her fellow sufferers, she did not talk about her past to her family. She kept her origins and the horrific events of her youth secret. However, the unprocessed trauma returned in her granddaughter's life, who tried to escape it by re-enacting the trauma.

All our families are full of traumatised ancestors who were maltreated, abandoned, sexually abused, persecuted or expelled. While such a declaration might at first sound extreme, as we learn more about our family's past, the clearer its truth becomes. However, if we are brave enough to face the lives of our parents, grandparents, great-grandparents, and even earlier ancestors, we realise how much pain, loss and fear there was, how many tears were shed over the course of their lives which would later be expressed in our fate. Unprocessed experiences, unmourned losses and broken relationships can all haunt us, waiting for us to finally bring them to consciousness. The first and most important step is to learn about them. The less we know about what our ancestors went through, the more likely it is that we will be impacted by their traumas in our own lives – and pass them on to our children in turn.

Traumatising incidents come in many forms, since in our lives we can be hurt in several ways: we can be wounded, rejected or abused within our own homes, or the threat may come from the outside world.

Let's begin with a wider, historical context – after all, the times we live in affect everyone's fate. Our private, personal life, our micro-story, is embedded in the overarching whole, so we cannot cut ourselves free from the events taking place on the stage of human history. Similarly, in order to reveal our family's history of trauma, we must learn about the age they lived in and discover what reality was like for them, which to us is just a chapter in a history book. The twentieth century in which our parents and grandparents lived their everyday lives was not short of suffering on a scale that affected whole peoples and ethnicities. War, genocide and the almost incomprehensible brutality of the concentration camps; revolution, resettlement, reprisals, persecution and executions – those times of bloodshed are just within our reach. Professional literature refers to these forms of trauma as *collective trauma*. In these cases, the individual shares the horror with thousands or even millions of others. If suffering is inflicted on human beings by human beings, if man becomes wolf to man, it is called *interpersonal* trauma. Natural disasters – devastating earthquakes, ravaging tsunamis, drought, famine and forest fires – are also a kind of collective trauma, but an *impersonal* one (not caused by human beings). When you are researching the blurred layers of the past, consider what collective traumas shook your family members, what horror they experienced, what cruelties they fell victim to.

Now let's turn from large-scale events to our micro-environment. It's a sad fact that most of us don't get hurt by strangers in the outside world but by the people who should love and protect us, in the place where we should be most secure: by family members, at home. Home is the primary location of *individual traumas*: after listening to many families' histories, I can say that they occur with shocking frequency. Abuse may appear in different forms. *Physical abuse* includes various forms of corporal aggression, be it a slap in the face, being beaten with a belt, grabbing and shaking a child violently, but also locking someone up in a confined space. While physical abuse is usually relatively easy to identify, the other form, *emotional abuse*, can often remain invisible to an onlooker – yet those who suffer it may carry the wounds for life. Being humiliated, shamed, blackmailed, threatened with the withdrawal of love and care, undermining a child's feeling of security and destroying their self-esteem may happen very quietly. Nevertheless, the devastating effect is clear. *Sexual abuse*, which according to trauma experts is perhaps the most serious, can cast a dark shadow over the lives of generations. This field includes not only acts involving actual physical penetration but acts in which physical or verbal boundaries are crossed, be it the eroticised touch of a child's body, the exhibition of genitals, or remarks about a child's developing body and jokes with sexual content.

In addition to 'abuse', which implies active deeds, *neglect* can also present a traumatic experience. In these cases, the injury is in fact caused by the omission of something. *Physical neglect* includes everything that assures and safeguards a child's healthy physical condition and development. If there's nothing to eat, no clean clothes, or even no clothes at all, if a child is ill and not taken to a doctor, if they don't receive necessary attention or medication – all these have an effect on not only physical but also psychological development. When we speak of *emotional neglect*, we mean cases where a child suffers a lack of tender gestures of love, care, concern and consolation.

Abuse can take many forms, but there is something all cases share, namely the abuse of power. Someone at the mercy of circumstances, usually a child, is compelled to suffer trauma before they are fully mature, before they are able to deal with the event or process it properly. In addition, they are most frequently abused by someone with whom they share a close emotional bond, someone whom they trust and look up to, and from whom they hope for protection and security. We mustn't forget, either, that the various forms of abuse very often appear together. After all, a physical slap not only stings the face but also causes a psychological injury, just as sexual abuse humiliates not only the body but also a child's deepest self.

Interpersonal traumas inflicted by people close to us — which are usually repeated over a long period — can cause enormous devastation. They poison healthy personality development and can erode trust for generations, distance family members from one another. They encode feelings of suspicion and an inability to bond on a cellular level, and ruin the ability to regulate emotions in a healthy way.

Spillover effects of traumas

> From the moment I arrived in this country,
> within weeks after liberation, I spoke of the
> camps to everybody willing to listen, and to
> many more unwilling to do so.
> Bruno Bettelheim, *Surviving and Other Essays*[4]

A young man suffering from anxiety comes to see me. It's his life's great ambition to be an actor – but there's a hitch. As soon as he walks onstage, he is overcome with nerves. He breaks into a sweat, gasps for air, and simply cannot remember the words. As he himself says, he is consumed by the dread of annihilation. Still, he cannot give up on his dream and keeps trying to perform with an amateur dramatic society. He cannot understand what drives him, why he is looking for the chance to relive that terrible fear.

These inexplicable, seemingly irrational acts often take us really close to a deeper understanding of ourselves. Whatever gives us no respite usually requires us to do something, although that may not be what it initially seems. For example, for this man, acting may not be as important as it first appears. My attention is instead seized by his symbolic representation of this feeling: he goes onstage in fear as if before a firing squad.

As I learn more about him, anxiety and tension seem to be quite familiar in this man's life. Indeed, they are so common that he doesn't even recognise it! He is used to this emotional state and thinks that everyone lives as he does, with a constant suffocating feeling in their throat. In his mind the world is a dangerous place where one must always be on guard to avoid trouble. He considers himself a rather distrustful type of person who doesn't make friends easily. He often feels tired and dispirited, exhausted by being on constant alert. He does not know what causes all this. When our symptoms become such an inherent part of our lives and we cannot name a single underlying reason, it is worth starting off some-where deeper. We should focus on the unconscious levels instead of our conscious functioning, seek out what memories, emotions and suppressed matters hide in the concealed corners of our psyche, which reveal by means of symptoms that something oppressive stirs in the darkness.

Katathym Imaginative Psychotherapy (KIP)[5] is an excellent technique for surveying the subconscious – a method worked out by the German psychiatrist Hans-carl Leuner. As its name indicates, imagination plays a vital role in KIP sessions. In a completely relaxed con-dition, the client increasingly focuses his attention on his inner world, while he calls forth from his mind images suggested by the therapist. At this time our 'intellect' (the cortical zone in charge of rational thinking) is at rest and hands over control to the deeper regions of our emotional mind. This part of our central nervous system communicates by means of images and symbols: it is there that emotions, notions, apparitions and swirling complex experiences hardly graspable by words lie hidden. In fact, we call on this area in the altered state of consciousness formed when focusing inwards, and we start plying it to talk to us. Leuner suggests that we start this work with the 'flower test': the type of flower chosen, its shape, situation and conditions reveal a great deal about the individual's connection with himself, the fundamental features of his personality, and his current psychological processes. In this case, we also begin with the flower image. After my client relaxes, I ask him to imagine a flower. 'It's a shell,' he says. I am surprised. I ask for a flower and he sees a shell? What could be the cause of this? On these occasions, many thoughts occur to the therapist. Perhaps he misheard my instruction? Did I not say the word clearly, or might my thoughts have wandered and *shell* slipped out instead of *flower*? I exclude these possibilities in a split second and reassure myself that the unconscious is always wiser than conscious thought: what I have to do is simply follow the stream of images. So we carry on with the image of a shell. 'I'm standing in the sea. The water comes up to my ankles. It is nice, clean and translucent. There's white sand under my feet. A scallop is lying in the sand in front of my feet . . . As if there was something on it. Aha, I can already see it! There's a tiny yellow starfish stuck to it!' Strange feelings overcome him; there is something suffocating in his throat, and the tension that he usually experiences onstage. Tears roll down his face. Then the image suddenly becomes blurred as if the sand had stirred and the scallop disappears in the dust.

We talk more after the flight of imagination is complete. He is shaken by what he saw, but it is rather the intensity of the feeling that startles him. He doesn't know what to do with it, is unable to explain it. As part of the therapeutic method, on such occasions we give the client some so-called 'homework', asking him to draw, paint, or make a plasticine model of what he saw in his mind's eye. This is also an important stage of processing what is inside before allowing it to emerge so that as a result it is easier and less burdensome to work with. In this process what matters is never the artistic value or perfect reproduction of the inner image, but the message represented in a symbolic way. When we next meet and I look at his watercolour picture, the story that the man actually has to deal with almost screams at me. Although he painted it, when I lift the paper and hold it at some distance from him, he looks at it with different eyes. I ask him, 'What can you see?' But the colour has already drained from his face. From this angle, the scallop's furrows resemble bars and the yellow starfish becomes an incongruous, disturbing and unmistakable symbol. The whole picture is painted over in light grey indicating the stirred sand, and the forms appear vaguely from underneath. As he begins to talk, his voice keeps faltering, and his family's past comes to the fore. His grandmother survived the war, aged barely three. Most of his family died in a concentration camp. He knows next to nothing about the details. They have never talked about it. The horrific events were taboo and always avoided. Only once did he dare ask about the past, but he saw such refusal in his grandmother's eyes and his mother snarled at him in such a way that he thought it best to be silent about it in the future. 'It was a long time ago, I needn't poke my nose in it, it's none of my business, not my story,' he calmed himself. However, the trauma he inherited lurked in his life, too.

When it comes to the surface, on the one hand he is relieved because he understands the deep cause underlying his anxiety, but on the other he realises that he cannot avoid facing up to the past and processing it. His grandparents' story suddenly becomes his own. He begins researching it, collects what information is still available, and they slowly start talking about it at home. The past that was haunting him invisibly until that point loses its strength by being spoken of, and not only he but the whole family is liberated from the pressure. From then on, they become palpably more open and honest with each other.

Patterns of pain, fear and suffering turn up in descendants who were not directly participants in the events. But how is this possible?

In 2014, a study was published in the journal *Nature Neuroscience* that caused an international sensation. Researchers at Emory University in Atlanta sprayed the scent of cherry blossom on a cage of mice while they were subjected to an unpleasant electric shock, causing the little rodents soon to learn to fear the otherwise pleasant aroma. Since Pavlov performed his experiments, we are no longer surprised by the phenomenon of conditioning, nor was this the reason why the paper became well known in the world's media. The researchers in this case included the *descendants* of the mice in the test. They found that the reactions of fear triggered by the scent of cherry blossom were also manifested in the second and third generations, despite the fact that they had never received an electric shock. More thorough tests showed that structural changes took place in the regions of the brain responsible for smell in both the first generation and the descendants. It was thus demonstrated that by being transformed to biochemical messages certain experiences – in this case fear and pain – affected the operation of the nervous system not only of those in question, but of their descendants too.

Such information transfers across generations are called transgenerational effects. Although they have only recently been reported in scientific journals, it seems as if the poet Árpád Tóth already had an inkling of them in 1923 when he wrote his poem 'The Rhythm of the Ancestors':

I am a man – new life, new traveller –
Who claims to be searching for fresh secrets out there,
Breaking a virgin path. But in me, quietly,
Thousands of ancient motions tread the old path.

Many old rhythms, thick and dark
Drifting in the body's secret depths,
Far from the light, yet steady,
Unfailing. And they tell ancient tales.

Who knows how many of my sad
Great-grandfathers lived with this unknown
World in their bodies – a world that exhausts
My rebellious nerve to weary gestures?

I would smile a new, gleeful smile,
But from the crimson bays of my heart –
From cell to cell – a bucket of dead tears
trembles silently up to my eyes.

With a fair new defiance I would defy,
But some primeval humbleness is now
Digging a coward's hole around my mouth,
A soft furrow, a gentle smile.

My forefathers, old, old vassals,
Are you still here? How many bad years
Shall it take for the weary offspring
To drag the stubborn troop of all those dark orders?

Are all the open roads a dream of drowsy sleep?
Is it impossible to start afresh?

Is there but one eternal command on earth:
To work and breed new slaves?

I do not think so. I have a little child
Of my own! And perhaps the ancient cell
In him shall be cleansed to rich joy, and
Forget all vague, old wrongs!

Oh, may the new realm of the pure
And happy come, a better new world,
And may the weary rhythms, the dead fathers,
Palpitate into a song in our hearts.[6]

Since evolutionary research tells us that all (or nearly all) human functions serve some kind of purpose, one might well ask: what possible aim can be served by passing on experienced feelings of harassment, fear and anxiety to subsequent generations? Why did nature arrange for the suffering of parents and grandparents to appear in their children's and grandchildren's lives? The answer, as always, is survival. Transgenerational effects can also be regarded as important messages that past generations send to their descendants to help them live well. 'Look what I've experienced in the world! Please prepare yourself so that you're not taken by surprise!' Yet, this inherited adaptability has a drawback. When the world becomes more peaceful — wars come to an end and the abuse of grandparents and the losses of the past are forgotten in the mists of time — increased sensitivity represents not an advantage but an inconvenience. What is helpful in times of trouble becomes a burden under more peaceful conditions. In order to stop traumas spilling over and to attend to our inexplicable, excessive or unjustified anxieties, we must face our family's past and reckon with our epigenetic inheritance.

At one point a woman with a kind smile came to see me. When we started talking, it turned out that her mask of serene informality concealed a great deal of grief. Whenever she had the chance of a steady relationship, she always fled. She could not really understand why, but sooner or later she always drew back and almost ran away from the budding romance. I asked her what she feared. Her answer? 'Being betrayed.' The word *betrayed* caught my attention: it sounded so strange in that context. I asked her what significance betrayal might have in her family. As it turned out, her father always warned her: 'Watch out: anyone can betray you!' Had there been any betrayal in the past? Did the word have a special message or remind her of anything? When she only tilted her head from side to side, I asked her to talk to her father and ask him what his belief was based on.

Next time, she came back with an interesting story. Her paternal grandfather took part in the civilian resistance in Hungary in 1944, yet one of his fellow fighters betrayed him, handing over the group to the far-right Arrow Cross. After they were caught, they were brutally tortured. Her grandmother was in the eighth month of pregnancy with my client's father. The expectant mother was terrified about whether she would ever see her husband alive again. By the time he was eventually let out, the once strong, good-looking man was but a shadow of his former self. His vitality was gone for ever: after that, he just idled away his time at home. He tried to suppress his recurring nightmares, the merciless memories of torture, with alcohol. He was a completely broken man. When he died, the family experienced only relief. But they did not forget the lesson. 'Watch out: anyone can betray you!' they warned each other, and the subsequent generations. Besides inheritance on a cellular level, words and frequently spoken verbal wisdom also maintain our ancestors' traumas.

Coded wounds

Genes, like diamonds, are for ever, but not
quite in the same way as diamonds.
Richard Dawkins, *The Selfish Gene*[7]

How do we receive messages from our ancestors?

In June 2000, media around the world reported the sensational news that the human genome (the complete genetic material) had been almost entirely mapped as part of the Human Genome Project. The fact that Bill Clinton, then president of the USA, and the British prime minister, Tony Blair, were happy to participate in the announcement indicated what a significant achievement it was. At the time researchers were convinced that our lives were regulated by genes. Not only did genes determine our physical outlook, they were also responsible for our emotions and behaviour; they directed what happened to us and what fate had in store for us. By mapping and sequencing the human genome, our future could be projected and the scope of our possible illnesses, as well as their potential treatments, determined in advance.

Of course, we now know that this is not quite the case.

It turns out that genes themselves only represent a basic code and do not tell us much about the extremely complex psychological operation of an individual. There is a relatively simple reason for this: genes cannot switch themselves off and on. They are turned on and off by environmental effects such as, for example, nutrition, stress and emotions. Or, if you prefer, they are turned up and down. These are called epigenetic effects.

Epigenetics is today one of the most rapidly developing branches of science. According to the immunologist András Falus,

> [. . .] epigenetics is the examination of a hereditary form of genes which does not involve a change in the DNA sequence. It seeks the answer to the question of what molecularly verifiable changes in the descendants' genetic development are caused by the effect of environmental factors on the parents.[8]

The prefix *epi* indicates that it is about mechanisms that are superior to genes.

But what could nature's goal have been with this mechanism? Let's take DNA first. DNA is an extremely conservative and stable structure that rarely displays changes. Even extreme environmental effects mostly leave it untouched. However, in order that an organism is able to react to current circumstances, thus helping its descendants to adapt better, a rapid-response mechanism is also required. Nature resolved this issue with epigenetic information.

Rachel Yehuda, a professor at the Mount Sinai School of Medicine in New York, suggests that nature prepares us to cope with traumas experienced by our parents with the help of epigenetic changes. This biological programme arms and prepares us for possible stressful situations. If our parents lived under adverse circumstances, if they were persecuted or regularly abused, if there wasn't enough food available for them, this preset stress system will help our survival.

So far it sounds very positive – yet if the danger passed long ago, this inherited adaptability becomes a disadvantage. People who constantly think they are in a war zone and who are terrified and racked with worry even though they are surrounded by peace and calm are more likely to develop various stress-related diseases.

This was precisely what Yehuda and her colleagues established in the case of Holocaust survivors' descendants, who were far more prone to post-traumatic stress disorder and, consequently, depression than those whose ancestors were not affected by persecution.

Keep it in the family

I'll tell you that I'm a monster, and a child is no
good for such a monster, and it was what my
grandad guarded me from. That's why he taught
me not to want a child. To break the chain. So
that I would not become like him.

Éva Péterfy-Novák, *Don't Undress
in Front of your Father*[9]

The great psychoanalyst Alice Miller's book *For Your
Own Good*[10] is regarded as a fundamental text about
child abuse. It makes for rather strenuous reading,
so I would not necessarily recommend it to sensitive
readers. This work, which was ahead of its time, demonstrates how the effect of traumas and deficiencies
acquired in childhood can remain with us throughout
our lives. If we become more sensitive to those cruelties that are so often suffered in childhood and yet still
denied, Miller states, along with the consequences of
those cruelties, we can stop violence being transferred
from generation to generation. I fully agree with this
thesis. Indeed, we must talk about the topic clearly and

openly in order to break the transgenerational spillover effects of trauma.

At a conference about child abuse held in California in the 1990s, John Briere, associate professor of psychiatry and psychology at the University of South Carolina, said that if abuse and neglect of children ceased, within two generations the DSM would shrink to a mere leaflet and prisons would be empty. Unfortunately, many people still do not recognise how fundamentally events in childhood affect our later lives. Like an underground stream, our early traumas keep appearing in adulthood and if we don't start treatment, they make not only our lives difficult, but also those of our children or even our grandchildren.

It was not that long ago that we realised on a social level how sensitive childhood was and how much it must be protected. Young children used to be regarded as miniature adults and people did not concern themselves with their particular physical and psychological needs. Corporal punishment and harsh treatment were seen as quite natural, and hardly anyone considered their negative effects. 'My dad used to beat me and it made me a man' is still often heard – and when it is, the question always arises: 'Yes, but what kind of a man?' It is time to recognise at last that abuse creates a wounded person, not a healthy one. We now know with certainty that physical and psychological wounds suffered in childhood leave an indelible mark on our entire life.

Researchers began to deal with the issue of child-hood trauma more seriously in the 1960s, but the first comparative study to receive significant attention was begun in 1995, headed by Dr Vincent Felitti and Dr Bob Anda. They surveyed 17,500 adults about their early years, and asked in particular whether they had what was referred to as Adverse Childhood Experiences (ACE). These include various forms of abuse (physical, emotional or sexual) as well as physical and psychological neglect. Felitti and Anda also examined whether the family was dysfunctional, whether the parents suffered from drug or alcohol addiction or mental disorder, and if violence took place in the family. The list also included prison time, separation and divorce of parents. Every affirmative answer received one point, and that was how they arrived at an individual's ACE score. Even an initial analysis of the data produced striking statistics about how common traumatic experiences really were: 70 per cent of the population scored at least one point, and 1 in 8 had an ACE score of 4 or more.

A childhood with painful experiences is, therefore, not a rare exception but the most common reality of the majority. However, the greatest merit of the research was that it clearly stated, at long last, the undeniable connection between childhood experiences and adult health outcomes: the higher the ACE score, the worse one's health. Body and soul suffer the effects of child-hood trauma, and these deficiencies are with us for life.

A few statistics: if someone's ACE score is higher than 4, the probability of depression increases four and a half times, the risk of infectious hepatitis and COPD (Chronic Obstructive Pulmonary Disease, including emphysema and bronchitis) is two and a half times higher, and attempted suicide twelve times more likely. And the sad sequence can be continued: the risk of developing lung cancer in those who had an ACE score higher than 5 was three times higher than those who did not experience trauma in childhood. A clear connection was also found between childhood abuse and frequent headaches, as well as sleep disorders. It was shocking, too, that patients with an ACE score higher than 5 and suffering from lung cancer became ill at a far younger age – on average, thirteen years earlier than fellow cancer sufferers with an ACE score of 0. Traumas in childhood unquestionably ruin one's quality of life, but they also reduce life expectancy.

When a young child is regularly abused, humiliated, neglected or exploited, it adversely affects all areas of personality development. It has an impact on the child's physical, intellectual and emotional development, and on their social functioning. Today, with the help of brain-imaging, we can see quite precisely what happens in the nervous system of a traumatised child. This is the most important point to understand: trauma not only means physical pain and tormenting memories (often stored only on a visceral level); the fear and dread accompanying threat and insecurity are not merely passing feelings. The long-term effect of trauma is based on the fact that the stress hormones 'marinate' a child's immature nervous system and, as a result, it goes down a different developmental track. This means that the structure of a traumatised person's brain is different to the brain of an untraumatised person, and therefore functions differently from the brain of someone fortunate enough not to have harmful experiences. When you cannot comprehend someone's behaviour, then, always think of the following: you are coming across a symptom of someone with an altered brain function. Childhood suffering also leaves an imprint on the macro-level. According to Felitti, who headed up the research, child abuse determines the health of a whole society and is thus able to influence the economic productivity of a country.

Why does maltreatment in childhood hold such great significance? Developmental neurology tells us that a child's nervous system not only matures according to an automatic biological programme: experience-dependent feelings also play an important role. What does this mean exactly? It means that everything that happens to a child, both emotionally and physically, will have an effect on the development of their nervous system – even (or especially) what they do not remember as an adult. According to perinatal psychologists (who are concerned with the earliest events in life), mother and baby live in a shared psychosomatic world, a so-called symbiotic reality. Due to this shared physical and psychological space, the emotional fluctuations of the mother (and, of course, the father) are of incredible significance and affect the biochemical processes in the child's brain. The parent's emotional condition shapes the child's emotional function, including the development of the nervous system.

Let's look at the brain of an infant or a young child. The task of the frontal lobe is, on the one hand, to coordinate the functions of the other regions of the brain and, on the other, to regulate emotional reactions. Emotions come from a low-lying region of the brain, from the emotional brain known as the limbic system. The frontal lobe holds back excessively vehement reactions, but, in a newborn baby or young child, this area of the brain is still immature. This is why a young child still expresses her emotions without control, screaming if hungry, and wailing when sad. Whatever tension she experiences, she cannot yet calm herself. To do that would require the (hopefully) mature nervous system of an adult. A parent is a child's 'outpost brain', which takes over the functions of the still undeveloped areas. The parent's presence is vital in situations of stress, be they caused by pain, hunger or loneliness. Although a child left on her own may stop crying because she gives up asking for help, she will certainly not calm down. If the parent can bear it and copes with the child's tensions, and is able to calm her down by rocking, stroking and keeping her close to their body, then, with time, the child develops her capacity for emotional self-regulation. But that time really is crucial. The predictable, sensitive presence of a parent who responds to the child's needs is key to controlling emotions and behaviour later in life. If the child has a loving and secure environment, over time the frontal lobe is wired up correctly and from then on does what it has to do – to put a break on impulses.

Now that we understand how sensitive a developing nervous system is, and how much it is at the mercy of environmental effects, the serious consequences of a difficult childhood may not be surprising. Abuse and neglect hinder the development of the frontal lobe, so an abused or neglected child will be unable to regulate their emotions, even in adulthood. They will be more irritable and short-tempered, and incidents that might seem insignificant for others may disturb their equilibrium in an extreme way. These adults wind themselves up and immediately hit the roof, freak out, quarrel, and are indignant in the case of the smallest inconvenience, and find it more difficult than others to calm down. They are like an oversensitive car alarm that is set off every time a large lorry passes by.

Where can you meet such people? Anywhere and at any time. Not long ago, I was driving along a motorway when I reached a section where one lane was closed. Drivers tried to move over into the available lane. Since I learned to drive in Germany (where drivers tend to stick avidly to the rules), I followed the merging procedures to the letter. However, another driver, who seemed to have missed this aspect, thinking I had gained an unfair advantage, stopped his vehicle in front of me, leapt out of his car, and burst forth with a few choice curses. I won't go into detail, but he even mentioned the oldest trade as my presumed profession. I had started to feel personally offended when I suddenly realised what I was facing, and so I responded calmly to his vehement outburst with the words 'I see, sir'. He was taken aback and stood there gaping. Then he gesticulated and said only: 'Fool!' On that point, we agreed. I did not want to get involved in an argument with him. Why not? Was I afraid, perhaps? Or did I feel his indignation justified? Neither. It was simply clear to me that the man was suffering from a frontal-lobe deficiency; he was unable to keep a tight hold on his temper and calm himself down. I'm sure the case I've described here is far from unique, because the inability to inhibit impulses is an everyday occurrence.

It is essential to note that those who do not develop the capacity for self-control, and are unable to regulate their temper and emotions, will be helpless as parents when they need to soothe their child's tensions. On these occasions you have no other tool than to return to the patterns of your own childhood, and therefore the reaction is irritation and aggression. That is how emotions and impulses can swirl relentlessly through generations.

*

Another tragic consequence of abuse and neglect suffered in childhood is that it prevents the correct interpretation of social signals. Those who were treated badly in childhood can form close relationships only with great difficulty, because thanks to their childhood experiences they regard the other person as erratic and unreliable. Moreover, they presume that the other wants to offend or attack them, even in entirely innocent situations. It therefore does not matter how the other person relates to them: a negative image is already set in their head and applied to whoever gets close. Their reactions are far more to do with this inner image (and addressed to the inner image) than about the flesh-and-blood person before them.

When Szilárd Borbély's novel *Nincstelenek* (*The Destitute*)[11] was published in 2013 it immediately became a literary bestseller. Most certainly a great number of people recognised their own or their parents' or grandparents' fate in the almost dispassionately reserved and dry sentences written from a child's point of view.

Our dad methodically beats us as men usually do. He has very strong hands from hard labour and they got tough from the heavy shovel. He rarely hits with his hand. He beats with a belt or whip. We are scared of our dad. [. . .] They beat us until we cry not only from fear but also from pain. So that we don't forget. [. . .] My mum said they thought they should do it because they were beaten too.

They usually say: 'This will make you a man!' 'You'll thank me one day.' That's how they finish beating.

Think about it. If someone lives through this day after day, how hard it will be to trust anyone and to believe that an approaching hand is not intended to strike but to stroke. Sad to say, I meet many people who carry this excruciating fate through generations.

Another woman in her forties comes to see me. Let's call her Edina. She is tormented and desperate because she has been suffering from sleep disorders for months. Although she gets to sleep quite easily, she wakes up after two or three hours and from then on she tosses and turns sleeplessly. Of course, when her alarm clock goes off in the morning, she struggles to get up. She is becoming increasingly irritable because of her lack of sleep: as she says, she'd 'even pick a quarrel with a tree'. Meanwhile she hates herself for being an unbearably hysterical and irascible mother to her children and a nagging, rejecting wife. She cannot think of anything that might have caused these symptoms to appear; she can't think of any reason which would even partly explain her sleepless nights. Meanwhile, problems are piling up at work, mostly because she is becoming increasingly indifferent and apathetic. She is simply not interested in what she does, and so she keeps trying to avoid her duties. Of course, her performance is beginning to reflect that. There's regular friction with her colleagues and conflicts crop up almost every day. When I ask her about the reasons, she says she somehow doesn't get on with anyone, she feels such a stranger. She doesn't have any friends either, because she finds talking to other people agony. She can't let her hair down; she doesn't let herself get involved in some situations. She says it is as if she were an alien who has just landed on Earth and doesn't speak any of its languages, or as if she were in an invisible cocoon that prevents her from connecting to the world. I can see her surveying and scrutinising me to see whether she can open up to me, whether I accept her or regard her as completely mad. When I ask about her childhood, she can hardly remember anything. She retains no images from the past: at most, small fragments. 'I can't remember' is her answer to nearly all my questions. We advance with great difficulty because whichever way we go we hit a wall. It is as if her life had not happened to her. Nevertheless, she perseveres – moreover, after some time she insists on continuing the therapy. So we talk, at first only about current issues, and we apply relaxation techniques.

Then one day Edina arrives in desperation. The day before, she went to the dentist and became unwell in the chair. She lost consciousness for a moment and then got worked up as never before. Her heart beat violently, she started gasping for air, and all her strength left her. She was totally shaken, mainly because she couldn't understand what was happening to her. We try to retrace, step by step, how she got to the point of feeling so unwell, but we don't succeed. However, the same thing happens again a week later. This time, as we've agreed, she watches out for tiny signs and as a result the pieces come together and we find out what lies behind these strange experiences. A scent is the key: the dentist's perfume, which was eerily similar to the one Edina's mother wore decades ago. Her mother (because from then on memories slowly come to the surface) treated her cruelly many, many times. It wasn't that her mother didn't like or neglected her: she tormented her. She made her work, gave her tasks, then demanded an explanation if she didn't accomplish what would have been too much even for a grown-up. If she made a mistake, it cost Edina dearly. A beating was on the cards using whatever was at hand: a wooden spoon, a slipper, a rolling pin, a broomstick, whatever her mother got hold of. Edina was little and could do nothing else but take it. While she was being beaten she imagined she was outside her body looking down on herself from the ceiling, or sitting in a distant cave in complete isolation. That way, the beatings did not hurt so much.

It takes months to put together the reappearing pieces of past incidents. She realises the extent to which the abuse she suffered at home alienated her from her surroundings. The idyllic family life presented to the outside world was so far from reality that she herself felt that she had to conceal how they lived. None of her classmates could visit her at home, and they didn't invite other guests either. The family hardly had any contacts and lived in almost complete isolation. Hiding became a foundational experience of her childhood.

She also finds an explanation for her insomnia. As she thinks it over, she realises that it all began around the first anniversary of her mother's death. Before her mother died, Edina had promised to fulfil her last wish to have a gravestone erected; her mother had wanted this very much, and for it to be done within a year. Edina agreed to the task, but it was not completed in time. She kept putting it off because she didn't feel like doing it at all. When her mother was alive, Edina had never dared stand up to her, and now after her death she was managing to put up some resistance, but the little girl in her began to dread recriminations. It didn't matter that her mother had died: Edina's inner mother-figure was still standing there with the rolling pin.

Edina managed to speak to a relative who provided some important details. They told her that her mother had had a terrible childhood after which she entered into a loathsome forced marriage. The only reason she married the man (who was far older than her and an alcoholic) was to escape home, where they treated her cruelly. She was beaten by her parents, just as her own daughter would later be beaten by her. It is hard for Edina to talk about it, but her tension slowly eases and her painful emotions gradually loosen their grip. Initially she is still very angry about her childhood, but later she begins to see her parents' fate, and her anger morphs into sympathy.

In order to rid ourselves of the haunting demons of childhood, we must see further than our parents. We must accept that they too were once helpless victims who passed on their unprocessed injuries to us.

I recently gave a presentation in which I touched upon the themes of childhood abuse and transgenerational transmission. In the Q&A session afterwards, a woman from the audience said that she thought it was a pity to dwell on the significance of abuse because it derailed our thinking. In her opinion, we ought to talk about positive memories instead of painting a dark picture of our families. I detected in her voice a desire to avoid and deny pain. However, matters do not cease to exist if they are not talked about: they must be talked about because they do exist. Breaking down taboos may be vital to protecting future generations from painful episodes in their lives.

A middle-aged woman comes to my practice. She is hysterically anxious about her thirteen-year-old daughter. Since the girl began to show signs of becoming a woman, every day has been a nightmare for the mother. What fantasies torment her? Day and night, she dreads that her vulnerable daughter will be taken advantage of, sexually abused or raped. She doesn't let her go anywhere on her own because she feels that her daughter is only safe if she is close by. It has already got to

the point that she has told her husband (her relationship with whom is, in any case, awful) to sleep on the
living-room sofa so that her daughter can sleep in
the parental double bed. I hardly have to ask before
she starts telling me what might be behind this almost
paranoid fear: a gut-wrenching history of sexual abuse
repeated generation after generation. When she herself was thirteen, her stepfather started to show a keen
interest in her. The increased attention even pleased her
for a while. 'I might have competed with my mother,'
she remarks. But matters suddenly took an unexpected
turn. One evening, while her mother was visiting relatives, her stepfather locked the bathroom door and
raped her. This in itself is horrible, but the story didn't
end there. She tells me that her own conception was
the result of a rape. What happened to her mother
eerily coincides with her own experiences: her mother
also grew up with a stepfather who groped and stroked
her from the age of thirteen, and then on one occasion when they were home alone he raped her. The girl
became pregnant and by the time she dared tell anyone
of it, the birth was just a few weeks away. And that was
how she was born. Her mother went from one unsuccessful relationship to another, dragging her daughter
along all the while, before eventually settling down with
the man who would become her abuser. Later, when
she was a young woman, she twice got into situations
where she avoided becoming a victim of rape through

sheer luck. Now she dreads passing this cruel inheritance on to her own daughter and feels vicarious fear
towards her husband, and all other men.

Research repeatedly shows that those who suffer
sexual abuse in childhood are more likely to become
victims again in later life. It is as if their protective
system is frozen: they often don't notice the signs of
danger so find themselves in similarly helpless situations. They regard themselves as incapable of being
protected, so saying no to violence becomes unimagin-
able. People who have been victimised come to believe
that aggression is a natural component of human relations, almost a necessary price to pay: that's just what
relationships are like and it's hopeless trying to do anything to change it. Unfortunately this idea can be passed
on to later generations. Several surveys have shown that
women who have suffered sexual abuse are less able
to protect their children effectively. This is one reason
why experts in trauma therapy consider it extremely
important for parents who've been abused in the past
to receive appropriate assistance.

However, we have to talk not only about abuse
but also about other kinds of physical and psychological wounds of childhood – after all, if they are left
untreated, they may cast a shadow over our children's
and grandchildren's lives. In his book *When the Body Says
No: Exploring the Stress–Disease Connection*, Gábor Máté
writes that parenting is 'in short, a dance of the generations. Whatever affected one generation but has not

been fully resolved will be passed on to the next.' Máté then quotes from *Heart*, Lance Morrow's book about his near-fatal heart disease:

> The generations are boxes within boxes: Inside my mother's violence you find another box, which contains my grandfather's violence, and inside that box (I suspect but do not know), you would find another box with some such black, secret energy – stories within stories, receding in time.[12]

We could of course express this in the language of biology: when our grandmother was abused, neglected or persecuted, the ovum from which our mother was later born was already in her body. That cell already sensed the increased level of stress hormones. The same is true for experiences during pregnancy, except that in that case *three* generations of cells are affected at once (the grandmother, the embryo of the future mother, and the ovum that will become the mother's future child). Many people have recently shared on social media the below image that clearly demonstrates it. The biochemical memories of our grandmothers' fears and anxieties live in us on a cellular level. Whatever happened with our ancestors, the traces of their emotions can be discovered in our lives, too.

In one of our group sessions, everyone was asked to draw their family tree: they had to find out who their ancestors were, if possible going back three or four

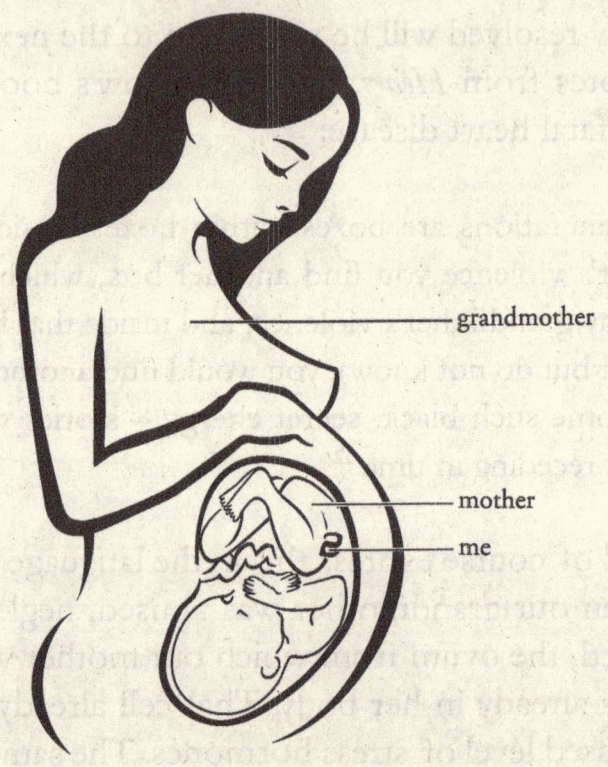

generations, and then present them to the group. A friendly, jolly woman resolved the task in a very interesting way, by arranging her whole family tree on one side of the page and leaving the other side blank. Of course, it was the absence that raised the group's interest. The woman didn't have the slightest idea what that part might symbolise, so we decided to 'stage' the family tree she had drawn in our meeting space. She placed chairs symbolising her ancestors on one side of the room and left the other side empty. Before long, she set off into 'no man's land' while observing her feelings. At one point she suddenly felt awful. She was seized by nausea, felt dizzy, and thought she was going to faint. 'What's there?' we asked her. 'Something disgusting and dirty,' she answered. 'Something you daren't even say, something that turns your stomach.'

Without overdramatising it, let me share some details of her family's traumas. The woman's grandmother was on the brink of giving birth when the war reached her village. Most of the women and girls had already found somewhere safe to hide. Her grandmother, however, had no such luck, and was found by Russian soldiers. She tried to run away, but with her swollen belly, she had no chance. Several soldiers raped her, after which they left the traumatised woman on her own. That very night she gave birth to her baby, but – still in shock – she was unable to look after it or feed it. For one and a half days she could only stare into space and listen to the baby's whimpering until it finally faded to total silence.

And here we uncover a fascinating connection. The woman now works in a children's home: every day she looks after, cares for and cuddles babies who have been abandoned by their mothers. She has recently adopted a little girl, in addition to her two biological children, because for her that was 'how life was fulfilled'. This woman seems to have identified with her grandmother's story and made her own life atone for the bygone tragedy.

Sadly what happened to this woman's grandmother was far from isolated: it is estimated that hundreds of thousands of women were victims of rape during the Second World War. In her book *Asszony a fronton* (*Woman on the Front*)[13] inspired by her own life, Alaine Polcz describes this tragic aspect of war, which had until then attracted little attention, in shocking detail; historian Andrea Pető's volume *Elmondani az elmondhatatlant* (*Telling the Untellable*)[14] presents a scientific summary on the theme; while the film *Aurora Borealis* (directed by Márta Mészáros and with Mari Törőcsik in the lead role) deals cinematically with the topic of rape, presenting it as an organic part of war.

Evolutionary psychologists who have examined the long-lasting effects of adverse treatment in childhood have developed an interesting theory. The basic principle of evolutionary psychology is that the primary purpose of our behaviour is successful adaptation: without being aware of it, we constantly seek the best possible means of survival in order to pass on our genes. Evolutionary researchers think that we do this by developing different life-history strategies depending on the environment. What does this mean in connection with trauma? To put it very simply: according to the laws of nature, children who live under difficult circumstances cannot be certain of their survival – their lives feel more precarious – and so they have to do their best to become adults as soon as possible, in order to pass on their genes. If circumstances remain difficult then the survival of the descendants is also precarious, therefore the more offspring the better. This strategy is called having a faster life history. In contrast, those with comfortable backgrounds do not feel the same evolutionary pressure and therefore they can choose a slower life history. And let's not forget: the strategy of each generation is passed on as unconscious knowledge to its descendants, who involuntarily organise their lives accordingly.

It is worth bearing this in mind when thinking about disadvantaged social strata and the transgenerational transmission of poverty. Disadvantaged people are often accused of irresponsibility, as well as of lacking long-term planning and perseverance. However, from the perspective of evolutionary psychology, families that spend their benefits quickly and put few savings away are doing nothing other than pursuing a faster life-history strategy. In any case, this wisdom has always been present in people's lives — just think of the proverb 'a bird in the hand is worth two in the bush'.

The wounds of attachment

'That's the way man is, *cher monsieur*. He has two
faces: he can't love without self-love.'
Albert Camus, *The Fall*[15]

Sigmund Freud, the founding father of psychology,
asserted that psychological health depended on two cri-
teria: the ability to work and the ability to love. We are
not born with these abilities. As we grow up, we have to
learn how to work, with persistence and motivation, as
well as how to be able to give and receive love.

But how is the opportunity to love turned into the
ability to love? Love is something like speech in this
regard. All newborns have a special sensitivity to voices
speaking in their own mother tongue, which they can
already hear in the womb. When they are born they
respond more vividly and positively when someone
talks to them in this familiar language. Their nervous
system records the information even though they cannot
yet reproduce it: they need to constantly hear, sample
and attempt speech. Children who for whatever reason
grow up without human closeness generally never learn
how to speak, since there is only a limited time-window

for doing so, entirely open at birth but gradually closing thereafter. If we receive adequate stimuli while the window is open, we gain the ability to speak; if not, this opportunity is lost for ever.

The most well-known case of this is perhaps that of Victor of Aveyron, who turned up on a French peasant's farm in 1800. The wild boy moved and behaved exactly like a little animal. People tried to speak to him, but he could not respond to human speech. When attempts were made to teach him, all efforts failed; Victor was unable to learn more than a few words. Joseph Sing, a missionary in northern India, experienced something similar when, in 1920, he found two girls aged between five and seven who had grown up among wolves. He tried to teach them, but these children were also unable to acquire speech. We now know that there is a crucial, limited period within which adequate stimuli must arrive in order for this potential ability of speech to unfold. In the absence of such stimuli, the system wanes and the potential is never realised.

The same is true – if not in quite such an extreme manner – of love, the ability to form deep and intimate relationships. This of course is far more difficult to spot than in the case of speech, but research results are quite convincing. The ability to love and be loved unfolds from the very early, visceral, physical experiences that we carry in ourselves unconsciously, and it returns in our relationships, as well as in the elements of our own parental existence.

To examine if and how the quality of care we receive as children affects us throughout our lives, researchers generally use rats or mice because their fast rates of reproduction and brief lifespans mean that several generations can be observed within one experiment. With these small rodents, one can clearly see which are the good mothers: those that build a nest for their pups and lick them a lot. Pup rats growing up with a caring, attentive mother acquire several advantages. Most importantly, perhaps, their nervous system becomes more resilient, and in stressful situations they return to a state of rest more easily – in other words, they are more balanced. They also have more courage to wander off and to explore – if they were people, we would say they were full of confidence – and they display greater curiosity about their environment, and even perform better in memory tasks. As for the unfortunate pups who are brought up by negligent or uncaring mothers – in brief, they lose interest. To put it scientifically, their exploratory activity decreases, demonstrating that they are uninterested in their surroundings. They lack sufficient motivation to discover their environment. In stressful situations they choose passivity, they navigate their way through a maze with difficulty, and they have somewhat deficient memories. If tender care has such clear advantages in these tiny mammals, how much might our fate be influenced by the quality of love, embracing and sensitive attention received in our childhood?

The first scientific studies of what happened to

children who are separated from their parents were made in the 1950s by John Bowlby, the father of attachment theory. Bowlby and his research team filmed children who were taken to hospital for medical treatment. At that time, parents were not allowed to remain with their children – after all, it did not even occur to people that this might be significant – and could only visit on certain days. One of the first films, *A Two-Year-Old Goes to Hospital*, shows a little girl called Laura in hospital for eight days. The child's transformation is striking. At first, she protests desperately when her mother starts to leave. Later on, she is angry with the mother; and then she reaches a resigned, apathetic condition, when neither her mother's arrival nor her departure trigger any particular reaction. But she does not only behave this way with her parents: after a few days, she is no longer interested in anybody or anything. It's as if she has given up the hopeless struggle to regain her mother and withdrawn into her own world to avoid the pain of being left in the future. When she is discharged from hospital after eight days, she doesn't really care. Five months later, when she is checked again, researchers find that the separation left lasting traces on the mother-and-child relationship. Little Laura learned, for life, that relationships are fragile and can be broken off at any time. She therefore followed her mother around everywhere, like a shadow.

One of my clients is a young mother with four children of nursery- and primary-school age. Her doctors

can find no somatic explanation for her recurring stomach aches, nausea and panic attacks, so she asks for an
appointment with me as a last resort. While we are talking, something begins to dawn on me. Although life with
four children is no walk in the park, I think there must be
a deeper cause than everyday exhaustion. I ask her what
she finds the most difficult thing about motherhood. She
thinks and then says that what she finds most difficult to
bear is that her children constantly miss her, because in
attending to one, she turns away from the other three.
The children continually and desperately compete for
her embrace and for her time, which upsets her greatly.
It breaks her heart that she cannot be present enough
for any of them. As she articulates this, she starts to cry.

We decide to pursue the theme of the absent mother.
Was her mother absent from her life? Did she ever experience her mother not being by her side? 'Oh, yes, many
times' is her answer. It turns out that between the ages
of two and five, she was often in a hospital far from their
village for weeks at a time with a chronic disease. Her
parents were allowed to visit her for a few hours once
a week. She has a single image in her memory: she is in
despair as she watches her mother set off down the cor-
ridor. 'What would you have liked?' 'To scream at her not
to leave me, to take me home.' Let's not forget: a child
of this age lives in the eternal present. Attempts by the
hospital staff to calm her by explaining that her mum will
be back next week, or that she will be taken home after
only five more sleeps, fall on deaf ears: such arguments

mean nothing to such a young child. Although my client does not attribute much significance to this past experience, the memory of separation is in fact fixed in her unconscious as a painful trauma. When her children cry and demand her attention, fretfully competing with each other, she undergoes a peculiar type of time travel without being aware of it. Her little ones' tension and stress 'here and now' immediately recall her own fearful experiences in hospital 'there and then'. In those moments, it's not the adult woman who stands there: in a split second she once again becomes the anxious little girl who was left on her own. Tension floods her body and nervous system as it did before and she is no longer able to respond coolly and reassuringly. She relives her childhood attachment loss in her own motherhood – and her children pick up on it and immediately adopt the nervous pattern. We should not forget that every period she spent in hospital as a little girl burdened her stress system, which in the end has become extra-sensitive. Stress has presumably left none of her cells unaffected and therefore it could have been passed on to her children via her ova. Physical and psychological processes might have imprinted her childhood memories of an absent mother in her own children's lives.

If a young child is separated from her parents – who are, after all, the main providers of the child's security – even if it is for an emergency intervention, there is a serious possibility of trauma. I must emphasise that it is immaterial whether we have memories about the absence that can be recalled and retold verbally: if our emotional attachment is repeatedly broken and for a relatively long period of time, our cells remember this throughout our life. When the trauma expert Bessel van der Kolk was asked somewhat sceptically whether these situations really leave a lasting mark on children's nervous systems and could truly be considered traumatic, he immediately answered in the affirmative. If a mother rat is removed from her pups every day, if only for an hour, there is a steady and detectable increase in the level of stress hormones in her descendants. If the mother-and-child unit is broken, nature will present the bill. When a mother (or caregiver) is present but is mostly unattainable emotionally because her own problems and difficulties prevent her giving her full attention, this does not fail to leave a trace. For children, psychological loneliness is no less destructive in its effects than physical neglect. (What will happen to the developing nervous systems of children whose parents are addicted to smartphones? From whom will they learn the ability of self-reassurance?)

Attachment surveys carried out by developmental psychologist Mary Ainsworth clearly show that the first thousand days after conception are crucial to our lives. It is during this sensitive period that we learn to trust others and develop a belief that we are good enough for them and they for us. If we are fortunate enough to be close to someone who is sensitive to our needs and who can be relied upon to take care of us, we are immersed in a wonderful feeling of primal trust that will accompany us throughout our lives. Our early relationships not only leave their mark in unconscious memories: they also influence the development of our nervous system. Our first experiences shape our physical and psychological development and personality as warm hands do plasticine.

The attachment pattern that is formed in childhood leaves a deep mark and returns in the relationships of adulthood. 'Tell me how you were loved and I'll tell you how you love,' said couples therapist Esther Perel in a lecture. Although it might seem bold to claim that early experiences of love affect what happens in our relationships decades later, recent research supports this notion, with attachment patterns in childhood and adulthood identical in 68–75 per cent of cases. It's worth remarking that while secure attachment in childhood can become insecure if affected by loss and troublesome events later in life, it seems to be more difficult to transform an already insecure pattern into a secure one.[16]

Our experiences as toddlers are so deeply ingrained that they significantly influence our most intimate relationships throughout our entire life. Early experiences, impressions and encounters become inner working models, guiding us without our having any conscious sense of how they work. We might entertain various rational ideas about the type of love we long for and how we would like to express our love, but if our emotional mind stores negative memories, they will direct the script of our relationships regardless of any conscious decisions we make. Our earliest memories lie behind so many broken marriages, fragile relationships and distrustful human connections. When someone is said 'to love in their own way', it is this attachment pattern that we are referring to.

These 'ways' tend to be passed on from one generation to another. Before a child is even born, we can already predict quite accurately how they will bond at the age of one and how secure they will feel in the world merely by talking to the mother-to-be about her own childhood. How a mother talks – her words, her hesitations, the sparse or detailed nature of her memories, tiny physical signals, the connections between and within her stories – outlines her unconscious emotional patterns. These will determine how she touches her child, her ability to manage and cope with stress, how much she'll be able to devote to her relationship with the child, and whether she allows and unconsciously assists her child to become an independent personality. The invisible emotional milieu of the mother's childhood becomes the inner core of her psyche. Her own absences and failings will all live on later in her motherhood. If she does not engage with her past and leaves her wounds unprocessed, they are likely to make it difficult for her sufficiently and sensitively to appreciate and handle her child's needs. Even if she undertakes all the practical tasks the baby requires, if she is not able to attune to the child emotionally, they will remain alone.

If we observe how our earliest experiences of love appear in our adult relationships – researchers most often use Mary Main's 'Adult Attachment Interview' – the most fortunate of us are undoubtedly those who are able to *bond securely*. This bond makes two important things possible for those who have it: we can become attached and committed while also maintaining independence. Since these adults were responded to sensitively and reliably in their childhood, primal trust was formed and thus they are unafraid either to give themselves to an intimate relationship or to keep their autonomy. They are ready to be committed but are also able to cope with periods when they happen to be single, or when their partner is not available. Their relationships usually last longer and are more harmonious. Adults who can attach securely are three to four times more likely to have children who attach securely.[17] These parents presumably attune to their children's emotional conditions more easily, and can usually provide the care their children need. It is also significant that they are more successful at soothing their children's feelings of stress, due to the effective regulation of their own emotions. Attunement and successful stress relief encourage the development of a healthy nervous system in their children. When I talk with securely attaching people, it turns out that they can recall many detailed memories from their childhood, which are mainly of warm and supportive families where conflicts could be discussed and where emotions, ideas and desires could be openly and frankly taken on board. Secure attachment is a gold reserve which we receive from our parents in our earliest years.

While international surveys show that around 50 per cent of us are capable of secure attachment, in my own country, Hungary – according to the Hungarostudy of 2013 – only 31 per cent of adults can be deemed so fortunate. In other words, nearly 70 per cent of Hungary's adult population has insecure attachment. This statistic must give us pause for thought.

While the basic experience of security does not vary much from person to person, insecure attachment can appear in various forms. Adults with *ambivalent* or *anxious attachment* direct most of their attention towards their relationships; we might say that they are addicted to love. They eagerly seek love and friendships that will last and provide security, but they dread refusal, being cheated on or being abandoned. As children they felt that affection and attention were unreliable (i.e. they sometimes received care when they needed it but sometimes did not) so they became hypersensitive to proximity and distance. They cannot be told 'I love you' often enough, because even after the umpteenth time they remain uncertain and in need of confirmation. Their inner, unconscious image of themselves is full of negative elements; their sense of self-worth comes primarily from outside sources and so they continually seek positive feedback from others. As a result, they often try to stay in a relationship at the cost of suppressing their own feelings. They tend to idealise the other and have a better opinion of them than of themselves. Their insecurity in a relationship consumes a lot of inner strength, and so it may cause them to lose control. If they are constantly agitated, if they don't receive adequate attention, if they fear being abandoned, they may become angry, demanding or even aggressive, before once again desperately begging for reconciliation and forgiveness. When we listen to how they speak about their parents, they turn out to be harbouring old grievances as adults, remaining in the immature emotional position of childhood.

Of course, one sometimes meets people who don't seem to want close relationships at all. How might they have been treated in childhood? Their emotional needs were probably neglected, and minimised with advice like, 'Don't make a fuss: big boys don't cry!'; or, on the contrary, they were over-reacted to, and a truth was thus encoded in their inner world: that emotions are dangerous and best avoided. A preference for independence as opposed to attachment is a characteristic of *avoidant attachment*. Proximity and deepening intimacy seem rather threatening to such people, who therefore try to keep their distance from the other, even in their closest relationships. They don't like 'heart-to-heart talks' or 'soul-searching'; they do not speak the language of emotions. We cannot expect thoroughly thought-out self-revelation or deep self-analysis from them: their inner world remains hidden from those around them. In cases of confrontation, they prefer to stay silent and try to get away from the situation as soon as possible. Work and accomplishment play the main role in their lives and they measure their worth by their success. Their self-image is mostly positive – they are the ones who say of themselves things like 'I'm a man of action' – and if they do have any doubts they quickly hide them from themselves. However, they do not have a very good opinion of others and exaggerate their smallest faults. When asked about their childhood, they are able to recall relatively few memories, and although these are positive, they provide a rather superficial and impersonal impression. People with avoidant attachment rarely see any connection between their childhood experiences and their adult lives, as if the past has no effect on them.

Disorganised or *fearful-avoidant attachment* is clearly the most difficult. The early experience of those with disorganised attachment is of hurt – that they were betrayed, exploited or neglected by the very person who should be giving them love and care. These words have no meaning in the homes of children who grow up with abusive or aggressive caregivers, or with parents suffering from mental illness or alcoholism. For these children, there is no relief or security: they are constantly afraid, every day. Will there be food, will their parent come home, and if so what condition will they be in? Not a single day is predictable – as if the family's boat were constantly adrift on a choppy sea, and where simply surviving is considered a huge accomplishment. Fear and dread are the most familiar feelings for them. They are obliged to take over the parental role in very early childhood, to care for themselves and their siblings as well as their parents, both physically and emotionally. As adults, they simultaneously want to be in a relationship and fear further harm. The disorganised type often experiences emotional storms: their relationships are characterised by a long-running tug-of-war, and they are happy neither with nor without the other person. Due to their insufficient ability to regulate their emotions, they easily turn aggressive and can even get into trouble with the law. Their self-image is negative, and so is how they think of others. When I speak to people with disorganised attachment, their childhood stories are fragmented. Listening to them, it's difficult to understand what really happened. They often cannot recall any memories before their teenage years — and if they do, they almost always consist of little else but one traumatic situation after another.

Let's not forget: attachment styles are largely built of unconscious elements, and are therefore chiefly discernible in the recurring patterns of our relationships. What I cannot stress enough is that every parent began their life as a child. When we think of the injuries inflicted by our parents, when shortcomings or a lack of attention or care come to mind, when we recall with pain their cold or demanding behaviour, we must remember that they themselves could only repeat the patterns of love they received. If those patterns were insufficient or damaged, they had little chance of passing on anything else. No one sets out wanting or deciding to be a traumatising, rejecting or cold parent. What they were able to provide as parents is the consequence of their earliest experiences of relationships.

In order to lead a truly free and independent life, so that the power of former grievances does not determine our fate, we must get closer to our parents' lives. We must discover what they went through, what baggage they carried, often from the time before their birth. If we learn about their past and understand the connections between their childhood experiences and their behaviour as parents, we can get closer to understanding ourselves. We realise that it wasn't our fault. We weren't the cause of what happened; traumas – perhaps carried through generations – determined our parents' behaviour.

Deeply engraved losses, fear, abuse and rejection may taint the animating feelings of attachment, security and trust for generations. Among traumas, the most painful are injuries inflicted by those closest to us. These are also the ones from which it is most difficult to recover, since we are actually afraid of what would help us most (as if someone who thirsts had a dread of water): the other person.

One day I was talking to a young couple who found living together extremely difficult. As far as daily routines went, everything was fine – but in tense situations (which, let's be frank, are not infrequent in real life), problems became evident. On such occasions, the man would withdraw and almost flee from home. It didn't matter whether he was having problems at work or was worried about some medical issue, he was unable to stay close to his wife. Instead, he would go fishing, which understandably drove her mad. She would have preferred to talk things through, but her husband wanted to sit quietly by himself on a riverbank, to hide. Why did he respond in that way? From his childhood memories, we learned that he was a colicky baby who cried a lot. When his parents had tried everything, but his screams continued unabated, he was placed under the big walnut tree in the furthest corner of the garden and left to cry to his heart's content. He would eventually stop crying, as if calm. Later, the family would repeat this story and laugh about it. It didn't occur to anyone that at such moments the baby might have been struggling not only with his stomach ache but also with the frightening feeling of being left alone. Did his mother mean to be cruel to him? Not at all. It wasn't love that his mother lacked but the capacity for secure attachment, which would have helped her cope with and calm the baby's tension. This case shows that clear-cut abuse or an intention to hurt are not prerequisites for something to go amiss and determine the quality of our relationships for life.

Now that we have considered the important role attachment plays in our lives, it is worth learning about the supreme significance of delivery and birth. Nature is a careful planner and has arranged for birth to be the moment when the neural circuits that connect mother and child are formed. The less disturbed the process is, the better chance nature has to do what it needs to do and attune the two parties to one another. However, an utterly undisturbed delivery is a rare exception.

Katalin Varga, head of psychology at Eötvös Loránd University in Budapest, demonstrates what happens when natural processes are unnecessarily interfered with. At the beginning of labour, oxytocin is released from the mother's brain. Some of it enters her body where it contributes to the regulation of contractions and helps to control bleeding, as well as stimulating lactation. This is called a peripherical effect because it spreads from the centre (the brain) to the periphery (the body). The oxytocin that remains in the brain floods the areas responsible for bonding, so that despite all the pain, giving birth can produce a captivating and elevating feeling that inspires the first waves of tenderness for the baby – at least, this is what would happen if nature were allowed to take its course. However, in 1953 something happened that fundamentally transformed the natural order of things: artificial oxytocin was produced. This was an important development because if a mother bleeds excessively during birth, oxytocin can help to ease the bleeding and thus a dose of the hormone administered by infusion is often life-saving. Oxytocin began to be routinely administered in labour rooms in order to speed up the natural process of birth: indeed, it is still referred to as a speeding infusion. This is the key point: if a mother receives oxytocin intravenously, her own production of the hormone ceases. What then happens is that the artificial dose is unable to break through the blood–brain barrier, so it does not flood the brain and does not have an effect. Without this very first burst of the 'love hormone', mother and baby cannot bond so easily, and secure attachment is harder to form, with consequences for the long term.

In one interesting study, mothers were divided into two groups: those with secure attachment and those with insecure attachment. Mothers in both groups were shown a picture of their baby crying, while cerebral imaging equipment tracked what was taking place in their brains. The mothers with secure attachment immediately had positive reactions and felt they had to do something to ease the baby's crying; whereas in the mothers with insecure attachment, the brain regions that were activated were those responsible for sensing violation of norms and for feelings of disgust – in other words, when their babies cry, mothers with insecure attachment initially respond with aversion rather than care. Like the mothers with secure attachment, these mothers provide for their babies, but for them bonding may be more difficult.

Creative ideas

'They are startled by my tear-stained eyes. They,
the happy, do not know what harasses me
inside, what stifles me so many times as if the
air surrounding me were thinning . . . I feel the
emptiness inside me, a part of my heart is not
filled . . . I am so good to everyone, yet no
one loves me! Lovelessness! your coldness is
more tormenting than the brimstone
of the damned . . .'
József Kármán, *Fanni's Legacy*[18]

At a psychodrama session, a woman who had been neglected and abused was working on her relationship with
her mother. As part of the long process, the woman
included this unusual utterance: 'Mum! I don't even
know who I am! You should have formed me!' How do
we, in fact, become who we are? Why do we think of
the world as we do? Why do some people think, feel and
respond so differently from us?

We are all born with terrific potential, with a psychological apparatus that is extremely open to opportunities
and experiences. Messages from our environment are

absorbed like liquid in litmus paper. At birth, we haven't a clue who we are. Just as we cannot sit, stand or walk, we do not have any images of ourselves. We first start to experience a sense of self through our relationships with another person (primarily our mother). As the Hungarian composer and educationalist Zoltán Kodály said, 'Not only does a mother give her body to her child, she also builds the child's soul from herself.' Kodály was not a psychologist but he grasped the essence brilliantly. A mother (and of course a father, too) regards the child as a thinking and sensitive being, and in the mirror of the parent, a child begins to learn who they are – which is why what they see there is so important. In a fortunate case, parents read their child's thoughts sensitively, understand what they want, and use this knowledge to decide what to do – i.e. *mentalisation* takes place. But what exactly does this word mean?

Before explaining, let me tell you about another case. A young couple were sitting in session with me. They had been arguing for several minutes and the atmosphere was turning increasingly tense. A tear appeared in the corner of the man's eye. His wife never even noticed it: she was furiously listing her grievances. I interrupted her and asked her to look at her husband and imagine what he might be feeling at that moment. 'How should I know?' she asked back.

Many conflicts in relationships are caused by such a lack of knowing and understanding, by the absence of mentalisation. A couple might live together but for many the inner world of the other is entirely alien to them, a terra incognita. Mentalisation is the ability to perceive the other's thoughts, feelings and intentions, which are different from our own, meaning that the question why our partner/mother/child has acted in such a way rarely arises. Similarly, we are also at home in our own inner world, and are able to name our feelings precisely. We not only say 'I'm on edge' but can distinguish between various types of tension and can identify whether it is anger, anxiety, fear or uncertainty troubling us. This has real advantages, since if we can give a name to our feelings, we have a better chance of adequately communicating and regulating them. If I understand myself, and also the other person because I can connect to their microcosm, then there will be fewer conflicts both internally and externally. It is really about knowing oneself and knowing others.

However, according to the Hungarian-born British psychologist Peter Fonagy and his colleagues, who developed the theory of mentalisation, we are not born with this capacity, but must learn it, just like a language. It is only at the age of three or four that children begin to be aware that what's in their head does not necessarily tally with what others think. With time, it becomes increasingly clear that another person represents a universe independent from us, and that we must constantly learn about them. Of course, sentences like 'I thought you knew' or 'I didn't think you'd mind' reveal that adults themselves often find it a challenge to make head or tail of someone else's world.

Researchers devised a neat way to assess where young children are in the process of developing their capacity for mentalisation. The children are told the following story:

> Max helps his mother to put things away. He puts the chocolate in the GREEN cupboard. He remembers exactly where he put it, so he can find it later, then he goes off to play. In the meantime, Max's mother needs some chocolate for baking, so she takes it out of the GREEN cupboard and uses some of it. Then she puts it back, not in the GREEN but in the BLUE cupboard. Then she runs down to the shop for some eggs. Max finishes playing and is hungry.

The question is, 'Where will Max look for the chocolate?' Children who solve the task correctly already understand that their internal processes are not identical with another person's thoughts, feelings and wishes. This will be the basis of their future capacity to be attuned to other people's minds. The implications of this simple experiment are very far-reaching: we need to understand each other to develop harmonious relationships. There's no point devising clever tests to determine our partner's 'love language' if we have no idea how they're feeling when they get home.

What is needed to feel secure in a relationship? Above all it is the feeling that we are understood even without words and that we don't constantly have to explain ourselves. And it is very important that we experience being understood without words in our earliest years – after all, that is how secure attachment will develop. Another of our major needs is to attune to another person so that their thoughts don't bewilder us. But what happens if what we perceive of the other from the inside is not pleasant? If their inner world involves destructive emotions, rage, anger, stress, aggression, rejection, or lack of love? On such occasions, there is only one option: to disconnect ourselves from the frightening experience and withdraw into our own small world. Many traumatised children lacking love protect themselves in this way.

Lack of mentalisation sets off a vicious cycle between different generations: the parent is unable to read the child's mind, the child does not learn to understand either themselves or others, and when they grow up they are unable to pass on anything but this lack. One generation passes on to the other the experience of psychological impoverishment and social isolation without having a chance to halt the spreading waves.

When the series *Patrick Melrose*[19] first appeared on television in 2018, a number of articles were published about childhood abuse. The most frequently asked question was how someone was able to hurt and take advantage of a child. Research suggests that some people cannot mentalise correctly and are therefore able to disassociate themselves from their victim's sufferings.

After the Second World War, both lay people and specialists asked themselves how the horror of the Holocaust could have happened, how people could have driven others to the hell of the gas chambers. The lack of mentalisation – 'mind blindness' – seems to have been a key factor. In the TV film *Nuremberg* (2000), the psychiatrist examining Nazi criminals says,

> I was searching for the nature of evil. I think I've come close to defining it. A lack of empathy. It's one characteristic that connects all the defendants: a genuine incapacity to feel with their fellow men. Evil, I think, is the absence of empathy.

Perhaps it's no overstatement to say that in contemplating the fate of descendants there are hardly any families where we do not find painful experiences, bewildering losses of relationships, and troubling incidents. Truly we are all descendants of traumatised ancestors – so let us track down and uncover pain that was concealed or considered forgotten in order to free ourselves from our oppressive shadows.

Questions:

- *Having examined your family tree, did any of your ancestors take part in wars?*
- *What do you know about those events? (If there are no stories among the family legends, history*

books, biographies and memoirs may help you with reconstruction.)

— *Did any of your parents and grandparents lose a relative in a war, deportation, genocide or other collective trauma?*

— *Did physical, emotional or sexual abuse take place in the family?*

— *Was anyone in the family neglected physically or emotionally?*

— *To what extent did you feel loved and accepted in your family?*

— *How much did you feel that your parents understood you and sensed your inner world?*

— *Were any conditions imposed for loving you and if so what were they?*

— *Based on the above, what kind of attachment style would you attribute to your parents?*

— *Which attachment style do you think is most like yours?*

— *Do you find it easy to attune to other people, or do you often wonder what they might be feeling or thinking and what their intentions are?*

PART THREE
Family secrets

There are three powers, only three powers
on earth, capable of conquering and holding
captive forever the conscience of these feeble
rebels, for their happiness – these powers are
miracle, mystery, and authority.

Fyodor Dostoevsky, *The Brothers Karamazov*[1]

The birth of a secret

Every story has a time to be told, I convinced
her. Otherwise you'll be forever a prisoner to
the secret inside you.
Haruki Murakami, *Sputnik Sweetheart*[2]

Family therapists think that every family has a secret
and that it is only a matter of time before it is exposed.
Some believe that families attend therapy hoping that
the long-suppressed or denied torments will at last
come to the surface. Of course, at first, they don't.
There is generally a symptom – a cover story, if you
like – concealing the secret. The symptom is a doorway
that can be used in the safe space of therapy gradually to transfer the emphasis to the real essence, so
that the truth can eventually be articulated and confronted, which usually sets off very exciting dynamics.
Often stating this truth openly and taking it on board
are enough to get things flowing, a bit like removing
the plug from a bath.

Of course, due sensitivity and caution are required to
bring a family secret to light, because if the timing is off,
if family members who were excluded from the secret

are confronted with the truth too abruptly, drastically or without due preparation, we may cause unwanted damage. As one of my supervisors once put it: 'There's a skeleton in every family's closet – but be careful taking it out, lest it fall and strike the therapy dead!' The psyche can only bear so much. If the condition of the psyche is not right, it first has to be made so: it has to be strengthened so that it can cope with the weight of the secret that comes to the surface. It is very similar to going to the gym: it's not wise to reach straight for the heavier weights because instead of becoming fitter you may suffer an injury. Just as we must warm up our muscles properly and increase the weight gradually, the soul also has to be trained to acquire adequate strength before it can face a secret. Truth that brutally confronts you can be as harmful as the lie itself.

This chapter is about secrets and reticence – about unexpressed and unacknowledged stories and experiences which we carry within ourselves for many years and often for decades. As Gabriel García Márquez said, 'Everyone has three lives: a public life, a private life and a secret life.'[3] We juggle these three lives of ours, trying to maintain control of them all while taking care not to 'drop' them.

Our public life is the one we show to the outside world. It is our well-bred and well-groomed self. When we step out into the world, we behave in a certain way. Our posture, movement, our way of speaking and even our voice change. In the presence of others, we automatically take care that the overall image is acceptable, that all our movements and manifestations match what we want to express about ourselves. The sociologist Erving Goffman called this *front stage behaviour*, whereby we protect our image.

Our private life is our own personal sphere. When we are with friends or family, we feel far more at ease and behave more freely than, say, at our workplace or with a group of strangers. We control ourselves less and don't pay as much attention to appearances.

The third, most intimate layer is our secret life. Very few can enter there – indeed, there are certain places perhaps no one is allowed to enter. This secret area is divided in two. On the one hand, there are things you don't share with anyone because they are no one else's business, only yours. You're entitled to your boundaries; you have a right to keep certain matters to yourself. I would not even term this a secret life, rather a healthy experience of independence. It is your independent, autonomous self. You might share it in an intimate relationship, but perhaps not even then.

On the other hand, however, there is a place in our soul where we banish memories, thoughts and feelings which we find unacceptable. That is where the real secrets are, secrets we deeply dread will ever be revealed. Just let them not come to light, let no one find out what we are really like, because if they did people would be disappointed in us, turn away from us, and in the end perhaps abandon us. There's nothing more worrying than the fear of suddenly falling into empty space, for our contacts with others to cease, and for us to be and remain alone. That is why we conceal and hide some of our thoughts and feelings, or perhaps what we've done to others or others have done to us. What lies behind most great secrets is shame, a scarlet letter that concerns our whole being – we are bad and unacceptable in our own eyes. And shame is passed on from generation to generation.

This feeling of shame that is formed in us is embedded in a relationship – that is, others teach us to feel it. The other person acts as a mirror, and if this mirror shows that something is wrong with us, that we are at fault and unacceptable, the pain of shame gets etched in us more and more deeply. This process begins very early in most families; a humiliating upbringing tends to go back many generations.

Children must undoubtedly be educated – shaped into social beings, taught how to behave and follow rules, as well as how to fit into larger communities. However, in our enthusiasm for this education we often trim their developing personalities unnecessarily, or cut into their souls so deeply that it leaves a mark for life.

Let's begin by considering the first and most general incident that usually occurs in families with young children. Children take joyful pleasure in discovering the world and themselves in it, including their bodies. They don't know that there are certain parts of the body that it is not proper to touch, especially not in front of others, and therefore they don't feel awkward about it. They take off their nappies and happily run around naked; moreover they touch their genitals or show them off without any inhibition. This makes parents who don't have a healthy attitude to their bodies increasingly embarrassed. They get more and more irritated as they try to dissuade their little ones from the indecent behaviour. 'Eurgh, no, don't do that! We don't touch ourselves there!' they say. All children eventually give up being naked, but in learning that it is not correct to be naked or to touch one's genitals in public they also learn that the body and its associated feelings of pleasure are shameful. The fact that 90 per cent of adult women are dissatisfied with their bodies, are ashamed, prefer to cover up, and would change something if they could, is hardly surprising, then. Men are not much better off in this regard: they too have plenty of doubts about their bodies and its functions, and this is also passed on from generation to generation.

A humiliating upbringing stems from the parents' own childhood experiences. Those who frequently heard 'Shame on you!' or 'What will people say?' in their childhood have learned that there are things you must be ashamed of and that people are observing them closely to see whether they are behaving properly. When they in turn become parents, their own childhood memories come to the surface. Although their position has now changed, even in a parental role they feel that if their child does not behave properly it will be to the parents' shame, and therefore they blame the child for what they used to be blamed for – everything that might cause shame. The patterns that are imprinted early are carried unconsciously, so though we may promise ourselves that we won't be like our mother or father, in the end we often catch ourselves reacting just as they did, using the same words that we heard.

This kind of humiliating upbringing is so common that it can be observed anywhere and at any time. For example, I witnessed it recently while in a queue in a pet shop, where customers often bring their pets with them. I was waiting for my turn in front of a little girl of about two and her mother, and behind them was a man with a handsome French bulldog puppy. The girl was very keen to stroke the dog, and the owner let her – the puppy, however, shied away from the child's sudden move-ments. It was still a puppy: everything is still new, which was why it was a little fearful and cautious. Seeing this, the mother said to her daughter: 'No, you're too rough! Even the dog is scared of you!' Wow – that really told her! I shifted from one foot to the other, and the child simply stared into space without moving. An unpleas-ant situation. I could not say anything – after all, I was just another customer; I can't start educating people. So I remained silent, although I would have liked to have told the mother that:

1. The little girl is not rough but an interested
   and curious person, otherwise known as a
   child. You should be glad your child is like that!

2. Puppies are often frightened because they are just getting used to life. It is perfectly natural and it is not the little girl's fault. (Incidentally, even if it had been frightened of the girl, it wouldn't matter: that would have been an excellent opportunity to show the child how to approach an animal gently.)

3. I'm begging you, please don't tell children (and if possible try not to even think) that they are rough because that will be imprinted deeply in their soul – and if it is repeated often enough, they will regard their desires and enthusiasm with shame. They will come to believe that if they are interested in something then they are rough, so they will temper their enthusiasm – which might lead to their joy, spontaneity and initiative being stamped out. Let them rejoice; let them discover the world; let them feel free! Even if we adults think that we must intervene because a situation may be dangerous – which this particular incident wasn't – it should be without rubbing their noses in it and humiliating them . . .

I would have liked to tell the mother all this, not forgetting that her reaction was simply an expression of her own past experiences. At some point in the past, she must have been judged and brought up to be ashamed.

The message is 'don't do what you want to because that's bad, forbidden and reprehensible'. That's how we start to make each other secretive – after all, a secret always concerns a relationship. We think that the relationship cannot cope with the truth. Where do we get this idea from? From our past experiences. From often minor situations where we thought that the other person did not accept us, that they criticised us, and we realised that there was no reciprocity or support in the relationship. At such times we'd rather clam up and show less and less of ourselves. There begins what experts refer to as the dynamics of a secret. If we experience hostility, refusal or disapproval, we think very carefully about what we can risk telling another person. In a rigid milieu, there can be no self-revelation. In such circumstances, we withdraw into our shells because we are afraid of being attacked, hurt, disapproved of or judged harshly.

To what degree a family encourages the development of one's own real self is soon apparent from its emotional atmosphere. All it takes to sense what this is like is to enter the family home. There are homes where the tension hits you immediately. Everyone is ill at ease and behaves artificially. They are preoccupied with front stage behaviour, even in the family circle.

When I was a child, we were invited to visit a distant relative. They lived in Budapest; we were the country relations. They felt it 'behoved them' to invite us; we could hardly say no. My parents probably thought it better to get it over and done with. As soon as we entered their home, our hearts sank. Their hall carpet was covered with see-through plastic, which was fixed to the floor at regular intervals with insulating tape. We had to tiptoe along it and into the living room, where the sofa and armchairs were also covered with plastic. This elderly couple lived like that: for them that was normal. They were sitting with straight backs and kept proudly offering somewhat dry sandwiches. I must have been perhaps seven or eight, but I will never forget the atmosphere, the stilted attempts at conversation, and my mother's desperate look lest I spill my orange juice. I had never been to a place like that before.

How many families still keep the truth hidden and under plastic sheets? How many people go home without having a chance to show themselves to those with whom they theoretically should be on intimate terms? How many wouldn't even think of expressing their fear and pain? How many are unable to share their deepest worries with those closest to them? The family therapist Virginia Satir stated that most families haven't even heard of open communication. They don't articulate what they feel or think, and when they get into an emotionally demanding situation, they either go on the attack, get defensive, become obstinate or silently withdraw.

Many things may become secrets, although the taboo secret is the most common. These secrets develop around topics regarded as social taboos, and are strongly influenced by the cultural and historical environment in which we live. However, it is not only society but also the family itself that determines what it considers a taboo. This includes everything that is difficult, improper, forbidden or not customary to talk about 'in our house' – shameful, unacceptable matters threatening stigmatisation.

One such topic in many homes is sexuality. Imagine the man who, decades ago, left his family for another man and from then on ceased to exist for the family. His grandchildren were told that he had 'gone abroad', even though everyone suspected the true reason; and now the granddaughter is so anxious that she suffers from panic attacks and can hardly work any more, but dare not admit that she is in love with a girl. This kind of repetition is not so rare. When a topic is kept secret from one generation to another, it often reappears, as if to signal its suppression.

Mental disorders are also difficult for many families to deal with – they don't dare speak of it, even with those closest to them. For example, a young client of mine started therapy after a series of infertility treatments. It wasn't until much later that she confessed to having mixed feelings about having a child. Her ambivalence was caused by her sister's mental impairment: at the bottom of her heart she was afraid that her future child might inherit the disorder regarded by her family as shameful. Although she went through the unpleasant infertility treatment, deep down she resisted the process. She didn't tell anyone about her fear because what was really wrong with her sister had in fact never been revealed openly even within the family. They pretended she was a bit unreliable and required more supervision, but a mental disability was what was written in the hidden medical records. Her disorder was the family's great shame that could in no way be fitted into their self-image. It was regarded as unacceptable and unprocessable, as if it were their fault. They didn't dare openly discuss the many difficult feelings and fears that had accumulated over the years. They struggled in silence and looked after her without complaint, but anxiety descended on the whole family system and prevented them from asking for help to at least make their lives a bit easier.

A previous marriage, infidelity, divorce, a child's paternity, an abortion, any form of abuse, suicide, alcoholism or death itself may become a secret – that is, any event which is accompanied by guilt and shame, fear of disapproval, and exclusion or unprocessable pain. All this is dependent partly on the individual and partly on the family. The fewer psychological resources a person or a family community has, the more unspeakable things seem. The more rigid and closed their system of connections is, the harder it is for them to struggle with events that might cause them trouble. Harbouring secrets indicates that there are unacceptable incidents, uncontrollable events, which are so demanding that they simply cannot be broached. 'What will happen if people find out? What will they say about us?' That's why there is silence: because it seems simpler. Silence, concealment and suppression transmitted from generation to generation are attempts to find a resolution. That's how keeping secrets grows into a family tradition. As a client of mine said: 'We never discuss anything in my family, apart from maybe whether the gravy's good!' In such families, appearances matter more than anything else. Avoidance and denial serve to maintain the family's perfect façade.

Of course, with any secret, it is difficult to draw clear boundaries between personal affairs, events that do not concern anyone else, memories and harmful secrets that poison relationships. What can I keep to myself, saying 'What's it got to do with anyone else?', and what must I take on board and speak about, however embarrassing or shameful it is, however much I regret what has happened?

The most important difference is that while a secret undermines trust and affects the functioning of the family system, a personal affair does not have that effect, especially not through generations. Another essential point is that shame, guilty conscience, and the inability to take an experience on board and to talk about it accompany a secret, but do not appear in connection with a personal affair.

Making something a secret is not really an active deed but a specific way of existing: it's not something we *do*, but something we live with every day. It is a permanent precaution and tense vigilance. It is a bit like walking through a minefield: one must proceed with extreme caution and remain alert at all times, because trouble may occur at any moment. People guarding an important secret that they fear might be discovered constantly keep watch over their environment lest an unguarded slip of the tongue or a tiny blunder betray them. Research has shown that guardians of such secrets usually think of them more often than the conversation actually merits. In the following section we will see how this affects our relationships.

The secret that separates

A human being is a leather sack full of secrets.
Ádám Bodor, *Labyrinths of Interpretation*[4]

When a family keeps a secret, it transforms the functioning of the whole system. On these occasions, boundaries are formed around the secret: those who know the secret are within the circle and those from whom it is concealed are left outside. It's as if the family was split into two different groups. The secret shapes subsystems and separates those who should belong together. A secret between people is like a chasm that cannot be bridged.

A middle-aged woman called Sarah turns to me for help after her father's death. She says she is driven mad by guilt, self-reproach and shame, and is tormented by pain. She has not eaten or slept since the funeral. She is slowly becoming a mere shadow of her former self. The story starts from when she was about eight and began to do athletics. Most often it was her mother who took her to training. The girl soon noticed (children usually notice such things pretty quickly) how taken her coach was with her mother. Then her mother and her coach began chatting and flirting. One day, after she picked Sarah up, her mother told her to go and wait for her in the car. From that day on this became a regular occurrence, and Sarah would wait in the car with her heart in her mouth – because what would happen if people found out what her mother and the coach were doing? And what would happen if they found out that she'd known all along? Sarah and her mother never discussed it. She didn't need to be told to keep her mouth shut. For years, Sarah was her mother's accomplice, dreading that the secret might be discovered. The distance between her and her father and sister grew and grew. The family broke into two well-defined parts – she and their mother; her sister and their father – the secret separating them like an invisible wall. For a long time she felt that her silence was a sacrifice she had made in order to preserve family life. But since her father's death it has seemed as if it was all a senseless betrayal for which there is now no hope of forgiveness. It takes time for Sarah to process and accept this dark shadow of the past, and to set her heart at rest, to be able to forgive her mother and herself for never having an intimate relationship with either her father or her sister because of the grave secret. What damage and loss happen in relationships in such situations! How large a burden it puts on a child!

It is a classical conflict of loyalties: if you take one parent's side, you betray the other. This early experience had an effect on Sarah's relationships, because she could never really trust someone to be faithful. 'I'm a traitor,' she thought of herself.

Often it is a single family member who has memories and stories that they cannot, dare not or do not want to share with the others. In these cases, too, the secret seems to be kept by creating emotional distance and setting up strict boundaries. People who try to hide an important part of their past from their families may feel that proximity and intimacy are far too dangerous – after all, if they allow themselves to relax or let themselves go, they might unwittingly spill the beans in an unguarded moment. Therefore they would rather avoid intimate conversations and hide behind the walls they've carefully constructed in order to keep their distance.

A client of mine said of her father that 'he was a loner'. They only found out at the Probate Court after his death that the quiet, reserved man had been married previously and had a child from the earlier marriage. Nobody in the family knew about it. The father tried to guard his secret past with the help of distance and isolation – ultimately, as it turned out, unsuccessfully. Who knows how many joyful personal experiences the family was deprived of, what deeper emotional memories there might have been involving the father, and, most of all, how different a model of fatherhood could have been passed on if this perfectly understandable (albeit initially shocking) secret hadn't been kept – because, it must be added, in the end the two families accepted each other and a very special alliance of mutual protection was formed among the step-siblings.

It is also not unusual for a whole family to hide a secret from the outside world – to lock it away so that no information can escape. When a family harbours a secret, the most secure way to protect it is if family members are kept under strict control. For example, the children are not allowed to make friends, they cannot invite their classmates over, and they'd better not go anywhere else either. They exist in a hermetically sealed world. I remember I was about fourteen when one of my classmates suddenly disappeared from school. She had always been an unsociable and reserved girl, and neither I nor my fellow pupils knew much about her at all. She never went on school trips or participated in after-school activities because she wasn't allowed to. Then rumours started to spread that for years her father had abused her and her brother, with their mother's knowledge. The family closed ranks and neither the frightened children nor the mother said anything to anyone. They took it for granted that it would only cause trouble and so they suffered in silence.

Each family has its own rules around communication. In a healthily functioning family system, family members by and large don't have to be careful and consider what they can say to Dad, what they are allowed to ask Mum, or what they mustn't mention in front of Grandma. In families harbouring secrets, taboo topics are given a wide berth and everyone is careful not to stray into a forbidden area. It is generally easy to sense where the boundary is between being able or unable to discuss something because as soon as a delicate topic comes up in conversation, a dark shadow seems to descend and the behaviour of the family members changes. It can even be detected without words – a sudden silence, a change in someone's tone of voice, facial expressions (say, a frozen smile), gestures, and even the depth and pace of breathing can all signal that a wrong turn has been taken. If you have grown up in such a family, you will have learned early on that your curiosity has to be kept in check and that you'd better forget about spontaneity. When you were a child, your parents reacted to your natural inquisitiveness disapprovingly or with hostility. Perhaps they snarled that you should mind your own business, or they looked daggers at you: you'd better shut your mouth!

In family systems where certain topics are made taboo or secrets are kept and open communication routinely discouraged, recurrent experiences finally develop into a system of beliefs showing that there are matters in life about which one must simply not speak. Although you often don't know the original secret, its theme is still forbidden. The following example perhaps demonstrates what I mean.

When Zita was a child, no one in the family was allowed to mention an uncle who had spent time behind bars. The children knew this without ever having to be told. 'It was clear that even saying his name was strictly forbidden,' says Zita, who is now in her mid-thirties. When he was a young man, the uncle had caused an accident in which three people lost their lives. The family was unable to process this: it left an indelible blot on the previously immaculate image they had of themselves. Mentions of the uncle and traffic accidents in general were blacklisted; family members could only make oblique references, and the black sheep was only ever referred to as 'you know who'. If a traffic accident was shown on TV, someone would immediately change the channel, as if the bad spirit could have wormed its way through the set into their home. It was only as an adult that Zita learned (from a distant acquaintance) what had actually happened. It turned out that the uncle was only partly responsible for the accident, which was why his sentence was not as severe as she had thought in her childhood. Growing up in this family atmosphere taught Zita two life lessons: mistakes cannot be forgiven and they cannot be talked about.

This is a poisonous system of faith that doesn't permit mistakes (which are difficult to avoid in life), and if one does happen to be made, there can be no absolution and it cannot even be relieved by discussing it. It is perhaps no surprise that Zita and her siblings have become overachievers who find it difficult to accept their imperfections. Constant agony accompanies their perfectionism, and they are anxious not to spoil anything. The dread associated with a fatal mistake has already appeared in their own families and has left its mark on their relationships with their partners and children. That's how patterns learned in childhood spread insidiously to the lives of subsequent generations. Zita still fights tooth and nail to maintain the appearance of perfection: when she has to come face to face with her husband's and children's weaknesses, she reacts with refusal and emotional isolation.

Distorting reality

[. . .] faith moves *no* mountains, but may
very readily raise them where previously
they did not exist [. . .]
Friedrich Nietzsche, *The Antichrist*[5]

Parents allow certain things and forbid others. They praise a child for one thing, but scold them for something else, and in so doing they shape the child's reality. When parents attribute significance to certain events while not noticing others, they demonstrate what is and isn't important in life. And children are like sponges when it comes to absorbing information: they are open to everything and take it all in.

Environmental factors shape children much like warm hands shape plasticine. They incorporate and accept their parents' way of seeing things. They identify with how the parents relate to the world and take on their reactions, using it to develop their own view of the world. So it really does matter how many secrets the family conceals and how important those secrets are, since children, whose attention is devoted to their parents, will inevitably run into the secret and become caught up in it. As they feel the world around them with their sensitive antennae, so they can tell if something is off. If we make out that a lie is the truth or hide facts that concern children, we create an alternative reality for them to which they can only adapt by making huge sacrifices.

A young couple's five-year-old daughter has been waking up with a start every night. She cries bitterly and it is difficult to calm her. Her parents are becoming worn down by their inability to soothe her. They would like to help their daughter and get to the bottom of whatever might be causing these night wakings. They want an explanation and a resolution. Their family life is fine: they both adore the little girl and cannot fathom what may have happened to their previously balanced and cheerful child. When a psychologist asks the girl to draw her family, she becomes engrossed in the task. She likes to draw pictures, so it's no problem for her. The picture looks like it's almost finished, with all family members present, when the girl turns the paper over and draws an extra figure on the reverse. 'Who is that, then?' she is asked. 'I don't know – but they're there,' she answers definitely – and the parents' hearts skip a beat. Yes, they say, or rather whisper, there is in fact someone else who belongs to the family. Before their daughter's birth, they had another child whom they lost when she was just five. That daughter had leukaemia and, in the depths of their hearts, the parents fear a repeat of that tragedy. 'We never speak about her, even to each other,' says the mother. 'We don't want to talk of the devil. We've avoided the topic completely.'

This case shows that speaking about our painful losses and daring to articulate our worst fears is not to 'talk of the devil' – quite the opposite. Memories we have tried to forget and suppress, fears we have tried to deny, burden our relationships. When we try to keep such a significant loss secret, when we think that if we never discuss it then the event can be undone, or we can avoid it happening again, we are grossly mistaken. The loss of a child cannot be deleted from a family's history – not even for those who are born afterwards. This little girl had the right to know that she was not the firstborn, that she had a sister who was lost. The information does not put a burden on her, but rather frees her from the burden of the unspoken secret. We are inclined to believe that if we spare a beloved person the knowledge of something painful, we will protect them from suffering. These parents' aim was also protection: to protect themselves from their fear and to protect their daughter from the thought that a little child can die. It's very rare that distorting the truth can fulfil a protective function, yet we still keep trying. We'd rather not talk about what troubles us, or stir up what causes us pain.

Although a life made artificially painless may at first seem attractive, it can in fact be immensely dangerous. A specific and rare genetic disorder comes to mind, in which those who suffer do not feel any pain, and so don't even notice if they suffer serious injuries. People with

the disease require constant supervision. Someone has
to keep an eye on them at all times, otherwise there is a
possibility that they might, for example, cut themselves
and start bleeding out without noticing. Being free from
pain imprisons them in a realm of constant danger and
increased caution. What they save on the one hand they
must pay double for on the other.

It happens similarly with the soul. If we are loyal to the
alternative reality, if a secret is fixed in the family's stock
of legends, a child's developing personality may become
distorted. The fabricated or incomplete family stories are
merely waiting to be rewritten and made true and complete.

Perhaps one of the most frequent and fundamental
secrets affecting a child's identity relates to their parentage. In the past, it was normal to keep the fact of their
biological parentage hidden from adopted children.
The adoptive parents often created a false history of the
child's birth and many even moved to another town in
order to reduce the danger of being found out. If anything can be described as an alternative reality, this is
surely it.

Imagine how many new fabrications, false statements
and misleading pieces of information this single secret
necessarily requires. At first the 'only' thing you don't
tell the child is that you are not their biological parents.
Then you make up a story about their birth, followed by
one about why they don't take after you, and so on. Just
as a stone dropped into a lake produces ever-expanding
concentric circles on the water's surface, the secret about

parentage spreads further and further. This is the prolif-
eration of a secret. Think how troubling this must be for
the parents, who have constantly to keep in mind their
whole web of lies. This fundamentally distorts the relationship between them and the child. Their entire family
life becomes dominated by their desperate attempts to
conceal the secret, and by the fear that the truth might
come to light.

I remember when I was four or five and it was suggested that one of the children at my nursery school
was not his parents' 'real' son. I could think of little
else for weeks. The hitherto unheard-of possibility that
someone's mum and dad were not in fact their mum and
dad completely fascinated me. But who were they, then?
And who was s/he actually? Besides the fascination, of
course, I also felt a growing sense of fear. What if I had
been brought from somewhere else and was not with my
real family? I started to ask my parents whether they were
in fact my biological parents. Poor them! They patiently
explained everything to me and repeated the stories of
my birth, showed me photos of my expectant mother's
large belly and others taken in the hospital, but nothing
convinced me. I became increasingly certain that they
were not my parents. When I brought up the matter yet
again – I was fortunate that in my family such a topic
could be brought up even multiple times – my father
said, 'Noémi, please put your thumb next to mine!' I did.
It was exactly like his, only smaller. It was clear as day.
'Surely you must see that I'm your father?' he asked – and

I did. From then on, I relaxed. Ever since, when I happen to catch sight of my thumb, I smile at my father's witty and effective genetic evidence, which has provided me with a feeling of security throughout life. And I've also learned how little adults know of the child's world of fantasy and fear.

Another secret related to parentage is when the paterfamilias is not the biological father. It's an extremely delicate and difficult topic, but examining its effects on the family cannot be bypassed.

Statistical data regarding how common this is are very contradictory. It used to be thought that as many as 20 per cent of children did not know their real father, but today far lower percentages are assumed. Sometimes the burden of this secret is borne by the mother alone; at other times the paterfamilias also knows, or perhaps even several other family members. One way or another, the secret of parentage will influence a child's developing identity and personality.

I meet Klári in a psychodramatic group. Anyone who has attended such a group knows the seemingly unmanageable human feelings of pain, disappointment, trauma or relations we often work with. In every session, Klári complained that what took place in the group was affecting her deeply. 'It's too much for me,' she would say, or 'I actually felt physically sick watching the play'; and indeed you could see that it really was difficult for her to confront such surging emotions. She responded with particular sensitivity to topics relating to sexuality:

she found these most difficult to digest. She remarked several times that she didn't think it was a good idea to dig down to such levels and that it would be better to proceed with caution. Then one day she arrived with the following story.

Her parents were moving to a smaller house, and she was helping them with the packing. While she was sorting things out in the loft, she came across a carefully concealed box that had in it her parents' marriage certificate and her own original birth certificate. As she looked at them, her whole body began to shake. Her name wasn't right and neither was the date of her parents' wedding. In response to her initial shock, she quickly closed the box, like someone trying to shut the genie back in the lamp, but then she composed herself to face the truth. She was lucky because her parents were willing to speak – uncovering the secret may have been a relief for them, too. Quietly and calmly, they told Klári that her biological father was not the man she had been calling Dad, who in fact had only come into her life when she was eighteen months old. Her mother had fallen pregnant while in an initially promising but ultimately short-lived relationship with a young man who disappeared when he found out she was expecting a baby. They hadn't heard from him since. In those days life wasn't easy for a young woman who had 'lost her honour', and although her parents helped her, she was subject to disapproving remarks every day. Then she met a man who was not prejudiced, and they got married. They decided not to stir up the past. The little girl wouldn't know a thing and they thought that would be best for her. They weren't really aware how many walls they built with that decision. Feelings, desires and fears were simply not mentioned at home: they mostly talked about everyday, practical matters, who had to do what and when. Sexuality was regarded as a particularly dangerous taboo, because Klári's mother always dreaded that Klári might get into the same situation. Femininity and physical pleasure were stigmatised as 'wicked and dirty', and it was deemed prudent to give these topics a wide berth. And Klári did just that. She was prudish and squeamish, not to mention reproving about everything concerning such matters. One could well understand how aggravating the drama group must have been for her – here the framework that had provided security was exploded. As the secret evaporated, so the pieces of her life fell into place. At last she was able to redefine all that she thought about herself, her family, and the wider world. She also understood why she so often felt excluded from the father–mother duo. While guarding their secret bound her parents closer together, it created a distance between them and their daughter.

Destroyed trust

'There are three honest things in the world, my
son: a young child, a drunk, and leggings.'
András Cserna-Szabó, *The Abbot's
Head is on the Line*[6]

Trust is a creative process, a construction. It develops with experience and repetition. Achieving it requires predictability, sensitivity and – perhaps most importantly – authenticity. We trust someone who is sincere and open, whose words match their emotions. Authentic communication forms a bond between two people. We feel good with someone who dares to be self-identical because we also dare to become ourselves. The families that are most conducive to their members' development, emotional maturity and personal fulfilment are those which succeed in creating an atmosphere of trust, where feelings can be articulated and taken on board, where there is no need for caution and events don't have to be shrouded in silence. Trust is the engine of growth. With insecurity, all resources are spent on survival and not on development.

A client of mine recently learned that she has cancer.

It's a shocking piece of news that has turned her world upside down. She is a single mother of two and she has no idea who she can turn to. She needs her family, the reassuring feeling that if anything happened to her, her mother and siblings would be there for her. However, she does not trust them. She is not even sure whether she should tell them she is ill. Where has the trust gone? Why isn't it clear that she needs their help? Why is she trying to struggle on her own?

My client's life story provides an answer to these questions. She is the youngest of three siblings. When she was ten, her grandmother died unexpectedly. The sisters were told that it was a heart attack, yet her elder sister overheard a conversation between their mother and brother: in fact the grandmother had hanged herself. The two girls never asked about it and pretended they knew nothing. In this case, the family split in two: a close relationship was formed between her and her sister, on one side, and between their mother and brother, on the other. A couple of years later, their aunt also committed suicide, and of course they weren't allowed to know about that either. Taboo, taboo and taboo. Everyone pretended that aunt also had a serious heart disease that had caused her death. Secretiveness became routine for the family: no one trusted anyone any more, since everyone knew perfectly well that they had deceived the other. 'You're not telling the truth, and I'm not telling you the truth about knowing the truth.'

When she later received a cancer diagnosis, my client

felt she had no one to turn to. In the end she managed to convince her family to attend a family therapy session, which fortunately worked out well. She plucked up sufficient courage to tell them about her illness and about her fears for the future. Her relatives were so shocked by the news that they decided to go back to the family therapist for a few more sessions to address their unresolved issues. Positive outcomes are sometimes possible.

Anita's father, a reputable lawyer, used to come home blind drunk every night. For years, her mother would rage behind closed doors and often brutally assault him, all the while maintaining for the outside world a pretence that they were a model family, upstanding members of the community. After some time, Anita also got used to lying. When she met a new group of friends, she made up all sorts of stories about her mother living in America, about a little monkey they kept in the living room, and about who knows what else. By the time she was an adult, she didn't trust anyone and no one could trust her. She was unable to truly commit herself to anyone, constantly putting on an act but remaining emotionally detached. Intimacy, revealing herself candidly to another person, was out of the question.

If people are asked whether they regard honesty as an important quality in a relationship, most say that it definitely is. We generally expect our partner to tell us the truth, so that nothing is left unsaid which might cause uncertainty later in the relationship. However, if we asked the same people whether they are completely honest with their partner, the picture would be quite different! It seems as though those who expect honesty and generally regard it as important cannot, will not or dare not speak openly about any number of things in their relationships.

The burden of a secret

Secret sorrows are more cruel even than
public tribulations.
Voltaire, *Candide*[7]

Most of the time we are unaware of how our language reveals experiences that are incomprehensible,
physical and visceral, or how our language reveals a
whole repository of encounters. For example, when
we describe a secret as oppressive, heavy, dark or poisonous we are expressing how it affects our body and
our whole existence, since a secret is in fact a weight
that must be carried. Imagine there is a weight of 1 or
2 kilogrammes attached to your body. Of course, over
time you would get used to it and stop noticing it, but
your body would change due to the extra weight. That
is how a secret affects us, too. The following experiment
illustrates this.

One group of participants was asked to think of a
significant secret; the other group had to recall an insignificant fib. They then had to estimate the gradient of
a mountain and the length of a section of road. Those
who had been asked to think of a more significant secret

always estimated the mountain to be steeper and the section of road longer than those recalling minor fibs. Those who keep secrets, it seems, find physical activity more demanding.

In another experiment, the participants were reminded of their secrets and then had to throw balls into boxes. Those who were thinking of a more serious secret aimed the ball beyond the target and exerted excessive strength, as if they were throwing a heavier ball or putting in extra effort. There is no question, then, that the body is affected by the process of secretiveness: it feels it and is burdened.

Those who cannot, or dare not, honestly articulate the significant stories of their lives find their psychological wellbeing reduced. After a while they don't feel good about themselves. For some time, it was thought that secrets cause psychological problems primarily because people usually try to conceal negative things, so whenever the secret comes to mind they have to confront something negative. Yet there is another factor: self-identity. Some people believe that a certain truth about them would damage their authenticity if it were not kept secret; they cannot accept it as a part of their real selves, and so they start to hide it. They are rather like adolescents who want to conceal their suddenly developing physiques with loose-fitting clothes. It is an immensely draining and frustrating process. Consequently, life satisfaction decreases: they might develop anxiety, high blood pressure, depression and a weakened immune system – the consequences for someone who feels that they cannot be fully honest might even include alienation and isolation. These days there are plenty of websites where anyone can share their secrets anonymously. To quote Frigyes Karinthy: 'I must not tell anyone | so I will tell everyone.' Popular sites such as postsecret.com or e-admit.com and various smartphone apps mean that when the wish to communicate the secret suddenly becomes overwhelming, you can do so immediately.

As Carl R. Rogers wrote: 'What is most personal is most general.'[8] We are not alone, even with our most deeply personal stories – the ones we consider most shameful. It is liberating to realise this. I remember a group where the participants had to write on a piece of paper, without their names, their most jealously guarded feelings that they would not want to be associated with. The pieces of paper were put in a box and then were read out one by one. Guilty conscience due to infidelity, hatred of an alcoholic father, feeling inadequate at work, feeling incapable of being loved, lack of self-confidence, an ambivalent attitude to a mother – such were the self-revelations written on the pieces of paper (which were then destroyed to protect anonymity to a maximum). That experience was shocking and, at the same time, liberating because we realised there was more that united us than divided us. From time to time, it does us good to be reminded of this.

Questions:

— *What was the emotional atmosphere of your family like? Warm, open and honest, or cold, isolated and reserved?*

— *To what degree could you talk and ask questions freely in your family?*

— *How was open communication encouraged?*

— *How was it restricted?*

— *Did you feel that there were topics it would be better not to talk or ask about?*

— *How did your family let you know when you had touched on a taboo?*

— *Are you aware of any important secrets that came up in your family or in earlier generations?*

— *Were you or any of your relatives ever made to feel ashamed in the family?*

— *Did you have any doubts concerning your parentage? Did you dare to talk about it with anyone?*

PART FOUR
Forming the family's fate

The issue, in a nutshell, is whether the first
person, singular or plural, is hiding at the
bottom of everything we say or think.

Thomas Nagel, *The Last Word*[1]

The birth of the self

> The past lives on in our movements, in our
> speech, in the way we run our hand through
> our hair. The time of our ancestors hides in the
> genes and lives on.
> Krisztián Grecsó, *Welcome*[2]

When the ego constantly asserts itself, it becomes ever more difficult to see oneself as part of a large familial unit, and especially to consider that our grandfather's or great-grandmother's lives may play a role in our fate.

Today, people regard themselves as number one – and also as number two! They concern themselves with their own needs and ungratified desires. They live within the magnetic field of their wants, and try to escape it by giving them ever more attention. 'I'm unhappy. I'm single. Love has gone. I have no motivation, no future, no belief.' And many add, 'I don't have a family, either: I cut them off because we didn't get on.' So, as Vilmos Csányi points out, we live in individual units and seek in vain for solutions that can only be found in connection with others – in relationships and in families.

Family. When I say the word, you picture an entirely

different image from the one my internal cinema presents to me. I see my father sitting at the head of the table telling a story, laughing heartily. We are howling with laughter and talking over one another; the family home resounds with our voices. A real Italian atmosphere. A feeling is also connected to the image: one of security, belonging together, joy. A family is not simply a community of people brought together by virtue of blood or law, but an impression of emotions, memories and experiences imprinted on a cellular level.

When I start working with someone, I usually ask them to close their eyes and think of a picture of their family. I ask them to tell me how old they are in the picture, where they are, who is present, what is happening and what the mood is like. In general, a good starting point for our work is the earliest social network of our lives: the family and its internal mapping.

Ferenc Pál, the Catholic priest, lecturer and writer, once told me about something that happened when he was talking with friends after dinner at their house. The children had already gone to bed when one of the daughters suddenly appeared in the kitchen. The mother asked her somewhat indignantly, 'What are you doing here?' The little girl answered entirely naturally: 'I live here!' This is the feeling represented by the family. 'I live here and not elsewhere; I belong to you and not to someone else' – and all this is beyond question. This feeling connects us with our fellow family members. We all know without hesitation whether or not we consider someone a member of our family – as if there were an invisible boundary between our family and the outside world. This remains the case even if, for example, you haven't talked to your sister for twenty years because she left you to do everything when your mother was dying. She is still indisputably part of your family – it's just that you don't happen to keep in touch.

We experience the feeling of '*we*' for the first time in the family. There's '*us*' and there are those who do not belong to the family, who are not part of '*us*'. A child aged barely two can already sense this separation, the boundaries around the family. They already understand that mum, dad, their siblings and their grandparents are not only independent people but parts of a unit. When I went over to a friend's for dinner, their three-year-old son greeted me with the words, 'You don't belong here!' He perceived precisely that an unknown element had turned up in the usual family set-up: someone (namely me) had barged into 'OUR' territory, and he thought that he was going to restore order. Luckily the parents understood the situation: instead of snarling at him or asking him to apologise at once because that's no way to speak to guests, they told him that he was right and that although I did not belong to the family, I was a friend who had dinner with them from time to time (and they with me).

It is our family experiences that first show us what different worlds we live in. I remember my daughter, about six at the time, pleading with me to be allowed to have a sleepover at her best friend's. She spent ages getting everything ready and nearly got cold feet, but in the end did go. When I went to pick her up the following day, she was unusually quiet, and only spoke up once we had got into the car. 'Mum, they're such a strange family! There is no bedtime story, and they only eat muesli for breakfast!' I think it was then that my daughter became aware of the different customs, rules or daily routines that characterise other families. When we live in a family, our behaviour and how we relate to one another become natural for us. We regard our family's ways as going without saying – and if we normally have Danish pastries for breakfast, we'll find it peculiar and strange to have muesli.

The experience of self-identity also begins to unfold in the family. Family members represent a permanent mirror: we look into their eyes and catch sight of ourselves. Since 'I' does not exist in itself and can be interpreted only via its relationships, our earliest experiences of how our family sees and treats us has great significance. If we're fortunate, family members reflect the image of someone who is loved and valued, lovable and valuable. If our fundamental experience is one of love and acceptance, we will be clad in strong psychic armour for the rest of our lives. However, if acceptance is questionable and love conditional, it will prove more difficult to develop our self-esteem.

In our belief

> It is clear that the family can make one very
> happy, or be an unbearable burden. Which
> one it will be depends, to a great extent, on
> how much psychic energy family members
> invest in the mutual relationship, and
> especially in each other's goals.
>
> Mihaly Csikszentmihalyi, *Flow*[3]

Every family is a miniature society with its own beliefs
and values, some conscious, some unconscious – for
example, whether existence is intelligible or meaningless. Are we in control of our life or is what happens
to us largely determined by outside forces? Are we safe
in the outside world or is it a dangerous and perhaps
hostile place? These beliefs are imbibed in infancy, and
therefore become so natural that questioning their truth
does not even arise. Andrew Feldmár says that parents
actually hypnotise their children: they filter reality for us,
and our earliest experiences come to us through them.
Their attitudes are our first model according to which
we build our own view of the world.

We may never have thought deeply about the effect

of the system of beliefs we grew up with. I had a client, an attractive young woman with a successful career, but who was not in a relationship. As she was speaking about her childhood, it slowly became clear what deep-seated beliefs she had. 'It's better to be safe than sorry' was her parents' recurring warning – and not only did they keep repeating it, they also lived their lives accordingly: suspiciously, distrustfully, without contact with friends and relatives. There was warmth in the fold, safety within the walls of the home, whereas beyond them lurked grim reality with hordes of people exploiting others. As she was growing up, that principal belief acted like a brake: as soon as she got close to someone, it was immediately applied, and it prevented her from having a steady relationship. She would say that she wanted a partner, but mistrust at a cellular level was always the stronger force. Our deepest beliefs about safety, the outside world and other people are unconscious. We perceive them only through recurring social patterns and characteristic reactions.

If a family is convinced that you must be afraid of the 'outside' world, and they convey the message, expressly or otherwise, that the world is an unpredictable and dangerous place and that life is a constant struggle, no wonder your gut reaction is one of caution. You will probably stick to your familiar surroundings and you're unlikely to set off sailing around the world. However, if your parents are open and interested, then the chances are that you too will approach new situations with curiosity.

A system of beliefs creeps under your skin unnoticed from childhood and determines how you will lead your life. For example, I recall a young girl who grew up in a close-knit family. Although she was happy at home, she had a rather dark image of the world. Her parents protected her from everything and tried to keep her away from new situations, overestimating the real danger. When in the early years of secondary school her class went on a two-day trip, she was the only one whose parents did not let her go. Eventually the time came when the otherwise brilliantly talented girl could no longer be kept within the secure walls of the family. When she was admitted to university, she did not realise how difficult it would be to overcome her fear of the unknown, which she had imbibed with her mother's milk and later with parental care. It took her a long time to realise that the view of the world she had brought from home was not set in stone: it could be reshaped, revised and remade.

Other families are convinced that the world is basically a good place, full of exciting and attractive possibilities, and we have a chance of leading a fulfilling life. With this attitude, even difficult life situations can be coped with more easily and turned to the direction of improvement and growth. Let me tell you the story of a very dear friend of mine, Dóri Pásztory. Dóri was born in 1984 with malformed arms. Having got over their initial shock, her family decided not to emphasise the issue with the little girl. They encouraged and supported her and let her find her own solutions: how to tie her shoelaces with just five fingers or to use scissors, but most of all how to lead a life which was about opportunities rather than limitations. Dóri became a creative and resourceful person. Thanks to her perseverance, she, the pride of Hungary, won consecutive gold medals in swimming at the Sydney and Athens Paralympics. Today she is a happy wife and mother as well as a great journalist. To have been born as she was in a tiny Hungarian village in the mid-1980s might have meant a life of endless compromise, frustration and disappointment. But that was not to be Dóri's fate, because her family's system of beliefs helped her to overcome these challenges.

Family boundaries

In the past a family's unity was based on
producing things together the family needed,
while today a family's activity focuses on
consuming certain things together.
Bruno Bettelheim, *A Good Enough Parent*[4]

If we regard our family as a system and begin to analyse events in that way, we can notice many valuable and
interesting things. Let's start with the issue of boundaries, which play such an important role in our life – for
example, the external boundary of the human body, skin.
It's quite incredible to think that our skin evolves from
the same ectodermal germ-plasm as our nervous system,
which is why it is referred to as an inverted nervous
system. I think that if Mother Nature has deigned to
develop our nervous system from the same small group
of cells as our skin, she has 'reasoned' that our external
boundary has a very important role.

Boundaries serve both to connect us to our surroundings and to protect us from them. Families also
have boundaries – two, in fact. One is the physical
border represented by the walls of the home; the other

is an invisible, psychological boundary, within which it is *us* and outside of which it is *them*. The saying 'my house is my castle' refers to these two kinds of borders. On the one hand, it expresses the absence of free passage between the home and the outside world. Every family can decide who they let in, since the walls of a castle are strong and only those for whom the gate is opened can gain admittance. On the other hand, it underlines that within the house/castle, our order, our rules and our customs apply. The handling of physical boundaries also depends on what psychological boundaries a family has, and what its members think of the world.

I remember once when I was in the first year of secondary school being asked to take the homework assignment to a classmate who had been ill that week. I duly went, taking a bar of chocolate with me, because according to my family not to do so would have been bad manners. I rang the bell and waited. And waited. Eventually, after a long time, my classmate opened the door – but only a chink. I had never seen her like that before: she was blinking, terrified of what I might want. By then I didn't feel too good because I had thought she would have been glad to see me and would have invited me in for a good chat, but instead there she stood and I could not even think of entering their flat. Confused, I gave her the chocolate and the homework, and, my enthusiasm having been thoroughly doused, I sidled away. Years later when I bumped into her, she told me that no one could ever come to her home because her dad simply could not abide strangers.

There is distrust behind closed, rigid boundaries. Threat and danger may come from the outside world, so we'd better watch out and not let anyone get too close. A few years ago, there was a TV series about American families preparing for 'the end of the world'. These families invested huge sums in accumulating stockpiles of food and water, but above all on super-safe shelters. They explained that the shelters would protect them from the hungry hordes who would be turned wild by the imminent apocalypse. Most of them were tense, their gestures and words expressed a high level of fear, although they talked about their efforts regarding protection very proudly, almost complacently. These were obviously quite extreme cases – but while only a few families prepare their own safehouse, many live in a sort of psychological shelter where they do not let anyone in. 'We'll be safe if we stay holed up here,' they think, and bring up their children in this spirit. Such a family is very fragile because if anyone gets into trouble, they are unable to ask for help or draw on external support systems and safety nets.

Yet boundaries exist not only between the family and the outside world, but also between family members. In an ideal case these boundaries are clear, and there is no need to think about whether they exist. Family members are aware how far they can go and respect the fact that beyond that point the private sphere of another person begins. At the same time, good boundaries are flexible: if circumstances require you can go closer than is customary to the other member. For example, an illness is one typical situation in life when even physical boundaries must be more permeable. When, say, a family member who has difficulty moving needs to be washed, the usual physical boundary is transgressed. Being sufficiently flexible to be able to adapt to the new situation is a good thing – and of course you have to be able to return to the original condition when the difficulty has been resolved.

However, in many families the *boundaries are rigid*. You must pay attention to what you say and especially to what you do; you cannot touch your father's desk except under 'threat of penalty'. An acquaintance of mine, for example, can only talk to her father, who has an important job, if she books an appointment in advance with his secretary – as if she were a total stranger. Such overly rigid boundaries prevent family members from being intimate. After all, who would feel like revealing anything to their daddy dearest at a time appointed in advance by his employee?

Excessively rigid boundaries also hinder communication. 'Don't speak, don't ask, don't even talk about it!' is, more or less, the message they send. Those who grow up in such families will find it difficult to make sense of their own emotions – if we don't learn in childhood that we can talk about anything, including our feelings, as adults it will be hard to express them verbally. And if we do not talk, our body will do it instead, in the form of symptoms and illnesses.

When a family labours beneath too many regulations, when the psychological distance between various family members is too large, the supportive function of the family is weakened. We should find it natural to turn to our family if we are in trouble, to phone our relatives for comfort, or to ask for concrete help because we know we can. But if we are used to keeping a distance, we'll be left isolated even amidst the greatest trouble.

Elsewhere it is *diffuse, blurred boundaries* that present a difficulty. Each member of the family is so involved in the others' lives and when something happens with a family member they react as one person. It is interesting how modern technologies promote the maintenance of such functioning. I keep hearing stories about family Whats-App groups in which everyone hears what's happening to everyone else several times a day. It wouldn't matter if the messages were about concrete events – where they've been, what they've done – but communication does not stop at this level. They immediately write if they've fallen out with their partner, if they've had a frustrating night out with friends – that is, their un-worked-out emotions are broadcast to the entire family. Crises come up week in, week out. Maybe the mother tells the 'gang' that she's considering divorce because the father came home late again; or maybe one of the kids left the group in a huff because her brother did not 'like' the photo she'd uploaded, prompting everyone to turn against the guilty refusenik. It is clear, isn't it, that a family with such diffuse boundaries is no more able to ensure a supportive function than a family whose boundaries are too rigid.

If we are fortunate enough, we learn from our family that our feelings can be shared with others, but the knowledge of how to cope on our own is also passed on. This is emotional self-regulation: you are able to calm yourself, at least temporarily, and you don't need to call your mum right after an unsuccessful meeting. Of course, this does not mean that you never tell her your news or ask for comfort – but calling her to feel better is one thing and doing so to avoid being swept away by a tsunami of emotions is quite another. On the other hand, if in infancy or early childhood your mother, father and other adults around you set a good example, by demonstrating both that emotions can be managed and regulated, and that stressful situations need not result in meltdowns, then when you grow up you too will be able to cope. It is in the family that the ability to bear emotional burdens is (or is not) acquired.

Diffuse boundaries make the development of an autonomous personality very difficult. A client of mine told me that it wasn't until she was at least twenty-five that she bought herself some clothes without her mother's blessing. There she was with a saffron yellow T-shirt, almost startled by her own courage. It made her realise that until then she hadn't even really considered making her own decisions. She simply didn't think it was possible. Her mother arranged everything for her, and she accepted her mother's decisions as if she were a puppet. She thought that that was the way of the world and that she had no say in her own life. She still has that T-shirt, kept in a drawer, and sometimes when she is feeling unsure or in need of confirmation, she takes it out as a memento of free will.

In this case the subsystem between parent and child was so diffuse and permeable that the child could not separate from her mother in line with her age. This brings another example to mind. A few years ago, I needed some dental treatment. At that time, many surgeries were rooms in domestic apartments: my dentist, for example, had his surgery in his elderly mother's flat. Once while I was in the chair, she came into the treatment room and asked him in the most natural way, 'Have you washed your hands, son?' It was so funny, I was in danger of swallowing the drill! However, judging by the look on my dentist's face, he didn't much feel like laughing. This example represents another rather diffuse boundary: the parent does not realise that her little Johnny is now in his mid-thirties and is a respected medical professional. Presumably she always treated her son as if he were an extension of herself and not as an independent person whom she should have kept at a distance commensurate with his development. In the end the dentist, who had had two short-lived marriages, bought an apartment close to his mother's where he now lives on his own.

These days we can observe an interesting social change. Parents who were brought up in the spirit of rigid rules and with respect for authority do not want to set such boundaries for their own children: 'Let them run free: no force, no restrictions!' The child is regarded from infancy as a partner and their opinion is consulted on everything. This marks the absence of generational boundaries. Children should not take the lead concerning adult matters: parents must do so, and that requires boundaries. As Salvador Minuchin, an expert in family therapy, wrote,

> Children and parents, and sometimes therapists, frequently describe the ideal family as a democracy. But they mistakenly assume that a democratic society is leaderless, or that a family is a society of peers. Effective functioning requires that parents and children accept the fact that the differentiated use of authority is a necessary ingredient for the parental subsystem.[5]

Let me put everyone at ease: children will pull through if they don't get to decide at the age of three which hotel the family should stay in on holiday. Appropriate and flexible boundaries transmit the feeling of security to them.

Minuchin also mentioned a dangerous yet quite common situation in connection with family boundaries. Children who surmise that their parents cannot properly perform their functions fully overstep the invisible but crucial boundary between them and become the parent of their own parents. It also quite frequently happens that this change of roles is initiated by the parents themselves who draw the child into the circle of adults.

Let's look at a real-life example of this. A kind woman with sorrowful eyes is talking to me. She is completely exhausted from caring for her bedridden mother. She doesn't want any help: she does everything. In addition, her husband has become frustrated with her paying less attention to him and has therefore given her an ultimatum: if she carries on neglecting him, he'll divorce her. 'I do my best, but I can't please everyone,' she says and waves disappointedly. I decide to focus on her efforts. Why does she think she has to do this? What has caused her to take on more than she can manage? 'I've always been like this,' she says. She begins to talk about her childhood: her alcoholic father whom they both feared and feared *for* lest a car hit him as he stumbled home; her exhausted mother for whom she represented the only support. She was barely five when she began helping out with the household chores. She remembers precisely how she was on the lookout to relieve her poor mother's burden. If needed, she cooked, cleaned and did the shopping on her own, pulling the heavy bags home along the ground. Besides physical work, she also tried to support her mother emotionally. When her mother cried, the girl put her arms round her, comforted her, and pleaded with her or encouraged her, saying everything was going to be all right, that she should not give up and should stick it out. Helping became her identity.

Later she became a nurse, the hospital's 'guardian angel' who always noticed if someone was under the weather or needed assistance. A special 'radar' had developed in her which could detect people in low spirits while others remained oblivious to their need. Meanwhile, she hardly looked after herself, since she felt good if she could exist according to the patterns she learned in childhood and could devote all her resources to serving others. She visited her mother every day, while still tending to the full to her husband and their adult son. This extremely exhausting yet balanced condition reached a tipping point when her mother became ill and she had less time for those at home. As her family history is revealed, it turns out that the story of women becoming adults early to serve everyone else has been repeated for three generations. They don't know any other way: a mother passes on the pattern to be followed to her daughter.

Parentification refers to situations when the direction of caregiving, support and security is reversed and children take on the role of their own parents. It represents a painfully early end to childhood, since children are simply overwhelmed by the adult world and have to shoulder a burden which they can hardly cope with. Specialist literature on family therapy shows that it can take place in two ways.

In the case of physical parentification, children perform tasks which are still too demanding for their age and physical strength: they cook, wash up, do the shopping, look after sick relatives, tend to animals, care for their younger siblings and accompany them to nursery or school.

Emotional parentification is when a child prematurely becomes a soulmate, a confidant and an emotional prop. A parent discusses their financial problems or conflicts in their relationship, reels off their woes, expects the child to mediate between themselves and their spouse or other adults. Sentences beginning 'Tell your father/mother that . . .' are instances of such expectations.

Taking on overdemanding physical or emotional duties too soon can distort healthy personality development. The child experiences conflicting emotions: on the one hand they want to meet the explicit or implicit expectations, while on the other, they themselves know deep down that they cannot fully perform the duties of an adult. As a result, serious disorders of self-estimation are formed in a child who otherwise seems precocious and smart. While they present a self-confident image to the world, the feeling of 'I can never be good enough' torments them inside. The parentified, protecting and supporting function is also fixed on a personality level, therefore later in life they often prioritise other people's needs to the detriment of their own requirements. Former parentified children can often be found in the caring professions, since they learned early on to pay attention to others' needs and demands and to selflessly support the downcast or the impaired.

Parentification is not such a striking or immediately apparent phenomenon and its dangers are not well understood. Indeed, the environment generally reinforces a child in the role of early adulthood with remarks like 'How smart you are!' or 'Your mum must be so proud that you can do it by yourself!'

Examining family functions, it is evident how intensively this mistaken role is passed on from one generation to another. When parentified children themselves become parents, they often expect their own children to support them from early childhood. According to family therapist Iván Böszörményi-Nagy, underlying this is a sense that since they were deprived of a serene childhood by their parents, they are owed a debt which they expect their own children to settle. Conversely, there are parents who, having had a miserable childhood, decide that they will do anything to spare their own children that fate – interestingly, their offspring will nevertheless follow the pattern and try to care for them. Unconscious models are more stubborn than conscious decisions.

Family stories

There are people with whom it is not easy to
live, but whom it is impossible to leave.
Thomas Mann, *Doctor Faustus*[6]

'Sometimes a person needs a story more than food to stay
alive' – so claimed the renowned American writer Barry
Lopez.[7] Our ancestors used to sit by the fire in the evenings and tell stories. That was how they passed on their
experience to the other members of the tribe; that was how
the next generation acquired the knowledge necessary for
survival. Feelings of affinity in the tribe and group identity
were reinforced and developed through storytelling.

As Vilmos Csányi states in his book *Ecce Homo*,[8] stories carry important social information: they are really life
maps that help one find one's way and show the right path.
Csányi also quotes the observation of Canadian anthro-
pologist Richard Borshay Lee, who spent years living
with Bushmen in the Kalahari Desert under extreme
conditions. Simply finding enough food for day-to-day
life represents a great challenge for the members of the
tribe. One might think that the Bushmen do little else
but search for their necessary sustenance; however, it

turns out that they spend only two days a week procuring food: they spend most of their time (60 per cent of it) talking. These are not scientific discussions or theoretical debates, but simple conversations about what happened to them while the others were away. A close community of Bushmen is able to ensure the survival of the individual, and in order to develop a close connection you need to know the other and be aware of what they're experiencing. Conversations are a source of cohesion, the binding material of the group.

Stories play an important role in family life, too. Family stories passed down through several generations not only strengthen relations among family members but also have significance in terms of their message. Essentially, the stories – by turns interesting, funny or tragic – convey an entire system of beliefs. They allow us to glimpse a family's values, how they relate to the world, or what patterns of relationship they have among themselves. A family story is a travel guide to life: it describes our opportunities, provides clues for resolving problems, and tells us what expectations we must meet. Stories guide our lives since without our realising it they teach us what we can and can't do. Even recalling the most mundane incidents can be important, because they capture the family's characteristic view of the world and pass it on. Stories are the family's way of interpreting the world. Children have as yet little idea of what the world is like: they learn about it through the stories and reactions of their parents and grandparents. Of course, not everything is included in the family canon. What is often retold is considered important for some reason, and recalling it regularly emphasises its significance.

If you think – because you've heard it a million times in your family – that life is nothing but a succession of trials and calamities, it will be difficult to imagine otherwise. Whatever good may happen in your life, you will struggle to be completely happy, because you always expect it to be undermined. If the message of the stories you heard in childhood was that you're better off not trusting anyone because people are selfish, then while you might have a different experience, you'll think it the exception that proves the rule – you'll simply discard whatever does not fit with your view of the world.

Family stories passed on from one generation to another greatly influence even the most common situations. An excellent example is the case of a woman who always struggled with the feeling that she was short-changed in life and didn't get her just deserts. When she went to a restaurant she always found something to complain about, whether it was because her portion was too small or because she was overcharged. At work she was constantly in conflict with her boss, who she thought miscounted her working hours and gave her disproportionately more tasks compared to her colleagues without even recompensing her. In relationships she often calculated what she gave and received, and lo and behold, there too she always thought that she invested more than her partner. It is worth spending time in therapy on a problem which regularly recurs, since it draws attention to some kind of essential psychological function, fundamental faltering, or characteristically distorted perception of reality. The feeling of being short-changed, cheated and put upon was so striking and all-pervasive that I decided to look into what was hiding in her individual life story, into what she had (if you like) in her transgenerational baggage.

When we began to deal with her family history, the roots of her negative attitude were soon revealed. After the Second World War, her grandparents' property was nationalised. Everything they had worked so hard for their whole lives long was taken away from them. The estate and the vineyard were lost and so was the mansion surrounded by mature trees – so, even, was her grandfather's beloved retriever. When they were made to leave their home, they could only take with them what they could put on a cart. That loss – the fact that something like that could happen at all – destroyed the family's sense of security for ever. My client, who was often with her grandparents during her childhood, heard them relate those painful events time after time with tears in their eyes. They told her again and again how unbearably hard it was to pack and how cruelly they had been treated by the people who oversaw their move – that they specifically mentioned. 'People are vermin. Vermin!' was her grandfather's summary of the events. You have to watch out for vermin, because you never know when they might take away everything again. Their granddaughter accepted this experience as unquestionable truth and built it into her own system of beliefs.

One of the most important features of belief systems is that they filter information from the outside world, only letting in whatever reinforces their existence. By accepting only what fits in with their worldview, they create an arbitrary distortion of reality. Furthermore, if anything contradicts the view you have developed about the world, you either don't notice it or actively deny it, since the security of feeling that you understand the world is often deemed more important than anything you might gain by overwriting your negative, suspicious system of beliefs. Thus for my client the balance always tipped towards the negative. This view of life was, of course, attractive to only a very few people; whoever could avoid her company did so. She gradually turned into a grumpy, lonely woman. We worked for a long time before the foundational tenets of her belief system began to crack. This example clearly demonstrates how losses experienced several generations ago and the bitter family stories about it can influence what happens to you in the here and now.

'Content analysis' is an interesting method of research increasingly used in the social sciences. In content analysis, researchers examine a given text to find which words occur most frequently and in what connection. By so doing, a text's hidden message – one that is not explicitly stated but lies between the lines – can be revealed. For example, content analysis has found that the number of words referring to ourselves in various texts (including advertisements, books and newspaper articles) has rocketed since the year 2000. These days words and phrases like *I*, *for me*, *about me* and *I see* are used more often than those that express connection and interdependence, such as *we*, *for us* and *together*. It's an interesting finding, and one that might support a sense that the world is becoming an increasingly narcissistic, selfish and egotistical place: the zeitgeist of our whole society, its atmosphere and the way people relate to each other, seems to be borne out in its texts.

The way we talk about a situation defines how we relate to it. For example, coming across a 'challenge' in life means something quite different from encountering a 'problem'. Although the event may be the same, we feel differently about it merely because of the label we attach to it. If it is a challenge, we mobilise our resources and want to find resolutions, whereas if we see it as a problem our approach is reluctant, strained or defeatist. A challenge is in some ways rather attractive, especially if we think we are able to meet it; while a problem repels us, and we'd rather avoid it entirely. Spoken words also affect our nervous system. A challenge stimulates and energises us at a cellular level, while the use of the word *problem* raises our levels of stress.

Content analysis as a technique can be brilliantly applied in individual therapy and today several such methods exist. When we start talking with a client about what words and sentences were characteristically used in their family, the milieu of relationships and the emotional climate they grew up in are clearly outlined. From time to time, the revelations that emerge are truly shocking.

A young woman who has lived on her own for years comes to see me. She asks me to help her find out why she is alone, since what she has asserted so far – that she has no partner because all men are fools – is no longer credible even to herself. (This is precisely the first step on the way to change: to realise that our existing explanations and judgements may not stand up to scrutiny.) It turns out that she has no problem meeting people and getting acquainted, but she always changes her mind when a relationship gets serious. At that point she feels she'd rather get out of the relationship because in the end the man would be a burden for her.

The topic of her ancestors is brought up and we talk about her parents' relationship: about what she thought of them when she was a child, how they spoke and related to one another. When I mention content analysis, which might provide a clearer picture about hidden messages within the family, she is so enthusiastic that as soon as she gets home she immediately digs out the family's home videos. For days she does nothing else but watch videos of past Christmases, birthdays and holidays, taking notes of any remarks with an emotional charge. Arriving for her next session, she declares, 'Now I understand everything!' When she was a little girl, she did not register the extent to which her mother criticised and belittled her father, the sheer number of disparaging and deprecating remarks she made about him. At the time she found it natural – even more so when she herself began to treat him as a simpleton for whom everything had to be spelled out, someone who could not confidently be entrusted with anything. The father, who was in any case a quiet, introverted man, had no chance against the two women, until in the end he even moved out of the family home and into a shed at the bottom of the garden where he lived on his own. As a child my client also found this quite natural, and never wondered about the underlying issues. 'My dad lives in the shed – that's just how it is!'

Of course, various explanations were given. Her father liked to smoke in the evenings and her mother didn't like that. He watched TV until late at night, which disturbed her too. But she never thought about the dynamics of her parents' relationship and how it might be connected to her troubles. The homework made her realise that she had absolutely taken up her mother's world of experience and that she related to men exactly as she had learned to do so from her. It is a 'psychological copy-paste' when you fit your parents' (or other important figures') way of seeing into yours without changes. This young woman's emotions regarding men were reflections of her mother's experience rather than her own.

Patterns of relationships we grow up with as children (for example, how our parents talk to, with and about each other) foreshadow what our adult selves will see as natural, normal and taken for granted in a relationship. If we fail to examine them thoroughly and follow them blindly rather than question their truth, we will not understand what's happening with us.

Family stories can also be life jackets and valuable resources in difficult situations. In her book *Fairytale Psychology in Practice*, Dr Annamária Kádár mentions some interesting research by two psychology professors at Emory University, Marshall Duke, an expert in family rites, and Robyn Fivush. Their research focuses on the social construction of autobiographical memory.[9] They wanted to find out whether a child who knew their family's history gained any advantage, if they had a so-called *intergenerational identity* – that is, they didn't feel up in the air but felt grounded as part of a larger family community spanning generations.

First, the researchers had to survey what children knew about their families, how clear relations in the family were to them, what old stories they knew, and how much they felt at home with the family's store of legends. For this they worked out a list of twenty questions, creating the following 'Do you know?' scale.

1. *Do you know how your parents met?*
2. *Do you know where your mother grew up?*
3. *Do you know where your father grew up?*
4. *Do you know where some of your grandparents grew up?*

5. *Do you know where some of your grandparents met?*

6. *Do you know where your parents were married?*

7. *Do you know what went on when you were being born?*

8. *Do you know the source of your name?*

9. *Do you know something about what happened when your brothers or sisters were being born?*

10. *Do you know which person in your family you look most like?*

11. *Do you know which person in your family you act most like?*

12. *Do you know some of the illnesses and injuries that your parents experienced when they were younger?*

13. *Do you know some of the lessons that your parents learned from good or bad experiences?*

14. *Do you know some things that happened to your mum or dad when they were in school?*

15. *Do you know the national background of your family (such as Indian, German, Nigerian, etc.)?*

16. *Do you know some of the jobs that your parents had when they were young?*

17. *Do you know some awards your parents received when they were young?*

18. *Do you know the names of the schools that your mum went to?*

19. *Do you know the names of the schools that your dad went to?*

20. *Do you know about a relative whose face 'froze' in a grumpy position because he or she did not smile enough?*

The survey was conducted in New York in 2001 and included fifty families who were visited in their homes to see how they behaved in their natural environment and how they talked at the dinner table. (I must remark here that in Hungary it is increasingly difficult to find families who still have dinner together, paying attention to each other. Meals spent together are slowly going out of fashion because people don't have enough energy to lay the table or enough time to sit down together, and it's tricky to coordinate the diverse daily routines of family members. Instead, when someone feels hungry, they'll just grab something from the fridge for themselves whenever they feel like it. Nevertheless, meals regularly eaten together represent an important form of psychological protection for both adults and children.)

Evaluating the results uncovered some interesting connections. For example, it turned out that the higher a child scored on the 'Do you know?' scale – that is, the more details they knew about their family history – the stronger their sense of self-esteem. This represents a really considerable advantage, since self-esteem in your life is like the foundations of a house: if they are strong and stable the personality will be resilient and secure. Those who have high self-esteem happily accept themselves and others, they acknowledge themselves as they are and are not anxious about their weaknesses.

The more stories a child knows about their family, the more firmly they stand on their feet, and the more protected they will be in difficult times. As Hungarian poet

Mihály Babits wrote in an essay: 'There is no future without the past, and the richer your past, the more threads there are linking you to the future.'[10] This is worth bearing in mind. The study also revealed that behavioural and anxiety disorders were less frequent among children who knew their families' past. These children believed in their ability to overcome the challenges they had to face. Not only did they not drift helplessly through life, they efficiently managed what was happening to them – and the feeling of being in control is essential to the experience of psychic wellbeing. This in itself would be important enough, but its positive effect can be seen not only on an individual level but also on that of the family. Families that talk about the past and tell stories about the old days function more harmoniously and healthily. They overcome obstacles more easily and are more successful at handling conflicts.

The attack on the Twin Towers in New York took place two months after Duke and Fivush carried out their analysis. That trauma became a common point in the lives of the researched families. The researchers visited them again to find out how the events had affected the children, and found that knowing the family stories conferred a great advantage in that situation, too. Children who knew their roots recovered faster and suffered less from post-traumatic disorders. Stories operated in their lives like the fenders of sailing boats: they protected them from the destructive effects of powerful collisions.

However, if you're thinking, 'Right, so let's forget

the French, maths and biology and fill the child's head
with some family stories instead, so they'll be protected
against the challenges of life!', I'm afraid it's not quite
that simple. The two researchers also realised that it was
not the knowledge itself that mattered, but the processes by which the child acquired it. Family stories are
not handed over in a nicely wrapped box in a single act:
they are retold and repeated on multiple occasions. For
example, when the family sits down to dinner, they don't
browse on their mobile phones or stare at the TV but
listen to one another. When they come together like this,
they naturally and spontaneously tell stories about, say,
Grandma's childhood, or when Dad first asked Mum out
on a date, or when one of the children was born. So time
voluntarily spent together, listening to each other, and
conversations in a relaxed atmosphere are all essential to
how storytelling becomes embedded almost unnoticed.
When a family is together in such a way, the nervous
system is flooded with a hormone called oxytocin
which, among other things, is responsible for developing
attachment between parent and child as well as in other
relationships. Almost as soon as it is released, we calm
down and relax, because the level of stress hormones
circulating in our body decreases. Oxytocin is a chem-
ical that really binds people, helping to develop feelings
of trust and stimulate social cooperation. So the recipe
is as follows: spend as much time as you can with your
family in as relaxed an atmosphere as possible. It might
sound strange, but it is scientifically proven that if you

tell stories and talk to each other, you'll soon feel better about yourself.

It's important to note that if you don't know certain details about your family's past, on no account should you make up a story for the sake of having something to pass on to your offspring – researchers strongly warn against that. False stories can in no way fulfil the role of true ones, and they undermine trust among family members.

At the beginning of therapeutic conversations, I often ask clients to write a family story which shows where they've come from, what memories, experiences and events are in their baggage. In this way, many interesting topics of self-knowledge come to the surface. We usually analyse the stories from several aspects. First of all, we look at the general forms of the narratives. As Duke and Fivush state when analysing the stories, three characteristic patterns can be observed.

There are ascending family narratives. These are usually about an impoverished or destitute family that worked hard and pressed ahead persistently, without losing heart, eventually achieving a higher standard of living. They encountered difficulties, of course, but always overcame them.

Descending family narratives, on the contrary, tell of how 'the family was exiled from Eden'. The characteristic storyline is usually the following: the family used to be well off but war, resettlement, economic crisis or some other calamity intervened and they lost everything. The prospects of reaching such levels of prosperity again are just castles in the air.

According to Duke and Fivush, the third and perhaps most fortunate type are oscillating family narratives. They are about the family having experienced both highs and lows and perhaps even very hard times, but eventually everything turns out for the better. The fluctuation of ups and downs conveys the message that there is hope, setbacks can be overcome, and we can stand tall again. For those who grow up with such a narrative, hope is fixed on a cellular level, which can be combined with effort. 'I act in this way because I believe deep down that it is right and for the best' is one of the healthiest approaches, which may help us even in the most miserable of situations.

We can also examine how relationships appear in family narratives. What role do others play in them? Are there friends who help, who can be relied on, who are supportive and stand by you? Or, on the contrary, do people represent danger, use you, and prevent you from achieving your aims? The elements of relationships in the stories show how you relate to people surrounding you: whether you dare trust them or instead have reservations about them. What you absorb in your earliest years in this field can be significant for your whole life.

It is worth thinking about how the family narrative relates to the issue of change and continuity. For example, does it promote development or does it, rather, warn you against seeking change and recommend remaining in a familiar framework? Does it encourage you to take flight while also helping you to feel grounded? For example, when an acquaintance of mine wanted to work abroad, he had to overcome the full force of the familial system of beliefs, which were holding him back. At home he enthused about the great offer he had received from the German branch of his company, yet he met with huge resistance. His parents tried everything to dissuade him; the situation went so far that they threatened to break off all ties with him should he leave. Their opposition reached back to a tragic event that had gained a specific interpretation in his family's legends. In 1956 a family member who lived in a small country town decided to leave Hungary. Until that point, nobody had ever moved away: everyone had lived in the same place for generations. 'We don't drift from one place to another' was a common saying in the family and they were proud of it. Then came the 1956 uprising, when 'people lost their minds, and everyone fled to wherever they could'. The young man did leave for Germany, but a few months later he lost his life in a car accident. According to the family narrative, 'If he had sat tight, he would be still alive!' The tragedy gave further reinforcement to the family's conviction that those who leave will come a cropper. In the end the story resulted in withdrawal: my acquaintance gave in to the family pressure and 'sat tight'.

Stories with important messages that are often repeated will eventually turn into myths. In cultures without writing, the telling of such myths is how ancestral knowledge was passed on to the next generation. These myths might be about heroic family members or about 'black sheep' whose unusual behaviour attracted the community's disapproval. These stories signal the opportunities of choice, but also inform people about the consequences: 'Choose wisely, because this is what might happen to you!'

There are also 'origin stories' which reach way back into the family's ancient past: where you came from and what your roots are. For example, I am often asked where my surname came from. People tend to assume that it's a double-barrelled name adopted after marriage – in other words, that I took my husband's name next to mine. In fact, Orvos-Tóth is my birth name. It is said that sometime in the mid-eighteenth century, the Habsburg empire was ravaged by a very severe cattle plague. Many animals perished and everyone was afraid that the losses would be irreplaceable. According to old documents and the family mythology, one of our ancestors tirelessly went round the country and helped to stem the epidemic by various means, and with all sorts of concoctions. News reached the Viennese court, where it was decided that such a noble deed should not go unnoticed: he was therefore granted the title 'Orvos' (Doctor), which was joined to his original family name of Tóth, and which his descendants have kept ever since. Although the recognition did not come with any kind of financial reward, we as a family can be very thankful for the 300-year-old story told over several generations. For example, no one in the family has ever doubted our innate ability to handle dire situations, or to offer help where needed. This story of integrity has become an important building block of our familial and personal identity.

Myths help develop and strengthen family identity. They emphasise what matters most, pass on fundamental values and help us to make sense of our lives. When someone starts talking about family myths, they disclose far more about themselves than they might think. It wouldn't be going too far to say, 'Tell me your family myths and I'll tell you how you are getting on in life!' According to research, the stories we grow up with and the worldview they encompass are in fact crucial.

Dr Mária Koltai, an expert in transgenerational transmission, has written about a meaningful example. Her research found that families with high incidence of suicide in several generations often passed on myths with destructive elements. What stood out in the narratives were the impossibility of change and the inevitability of tragedy – as if the ancestors were sending a message that we have no choices in the world and problems cannot be resolved. If you were in a difficult situation, self-destruction was the only possible way.

Stories seem to be able to contribute to the development of psychological disorders. Professor Bernadette Péley, an expert in narrative psychology, says that if, for example, the difference between the experienced and the narrated past is too large – that is, if too many untrue elements are included in a story – it contributes considerably to the development of mental disorders. If speech deceives, the soul suffers.

Tasks, questions:

- *Collect often-repeated stories in your family.*
- *Note the direction the stories take. Are they ascending, descending or oscillating narratives?*
- *What important truth(s) about life do they pass on?*
- *Which stories dominate the family's store of legends?*
- *What values do the stories pass on?*
- *What do they suggest about the family's self-image?*
- *What do they say about change? Is there opportunity for change or do they emphasise the impossibility of change?*
- *To what extent does the family narrative accept geographical mobility? Is moving good, a way forward, or does it happen only out of necessity?*
- *What careers does the family narrative regard as possible? (For example, 'All the men in our family are lawyers: you'll probably be one too . . .')*
- *Do the family stories regard studying as valuable?*
- *What do the stories tell you about getting on in life? 'Study because that's the way forward', 'Work hard because that is the only way to hold your ground' or 'Only the skilful survive'?*

PART FIVE

In the wake of inheritance

'At a certain stage one is inclined to think
everyone knows a little more than they are
willing to tell you.'
'They usually do, too [. . .] Only, it quite often
isn't anything to do with the business in hand.
It's some family peccadillo or some silly scrape
that people are afraid is going to be dragged
into the open.'
Agatha Christie, *4:50 from Paddington*[1]

The familial unconscious

a song of love a song of death
forgive us our fathers' debts
my roaring words are chiming bells
golden sticks in beggars' hands
Ferenc Birtalan, 'Inheritance'[2]

It does not matter how old you are, how far you live from your family, or how much or how little you know about them, they are always present in your life. They hold your hand invisibly and pull you along with them on the path they have marked out. Many people feel that life just happens to them: that their efforts are all in vain, and that they cannot control events. They drift along, taking little joy in their everyday life, and experiencing all the more tension, annoyance and frustration. In the middle of their lives, they look round apathetically: romances losing their spark, dull or demanding jobs, illness, using alcohol or other substances to numb their disappointment. In a large number of cases this is an expression of unprocessed difficulties, unmourned losses and painful traumas that have been passed on by previous generations. As long as the past remains unexamined, you have no choice but to suffer helplessly and console yourself by saying, 'That's life.' In fact, life grants you a much larger playing field than you'd think, but to make the most of it, we have to learn about our family's past and put the pieces together like a puzzle. These pieces of our ancestors' lives are part of the entirety of our own fate.

This is exactly why many of us eventually feel a pressing need to understand why our fate has developed as it has, why we've made the decisions we have, and what kind of inner compass we have followed in order to go forward. On these occasions we also ponder to what extent our story 'has already been written' and whether we have had an opportunity to exercise free choice.

These were the questions occupying the internationally renowned neurologist and psychiatrist Lipót Szondi when he developed his theory of 'fate analysis'. Szondi thought that our fate was no less than an endless series of choices: we choose a partner, a friend, an occupation, but also illness and even death. His theory was that these decisions are directed by an invisible force, the 'familial unconscious'. (While Freud enriched the science of psychology with the individual unconscious and Jung did so with the collective unconscious, Szondi drew attention to the unconscious inclinations hiding in the depths of the familial system.) He thought that our ancestors offered various possibilities of fate among which we ourselves chose what to accept and make part of our life and what to reject. However, in order to be able to do this consciously and freely, we must bring our familial inheritance from unknown obscurity to light and in full knowledge decide what to take on and what to let go. We can only completely understand our fate by uncovering our family history and our transgenerational inheritance, and in so doing take the governance of our life into our own hands.

This became obvious to me when I experienced an emotional shock with roots in my family's history. For me, the cathartic recognition was connected to the birth of my daughter. It was winter, a frosty Saturday in January, when we arrived home from the hospital with the sniffling little bundle, barely a week old. After I put my daughter in her cot, I stood above her for a moment admiring her, listening to her breathing peacefully as she slept. And then a terrible feeling rent my idyll: *I could lose this child.* It was like an excruciating electric shock: it quite knocked me out. It was at around this time that I began my studies in psychology at Eötvös Loránd University in Budapest. I knew a bit about how sudden postnatal hormonal changes can cause a depressive mood in many women, yet I felt clearly that in my case it was about more than that. I simply knew that the bulk of that fear was not mine; it was not about me. Of course, at that particular moment I did not have the complete picture, but from then on I was tormented by what might have happened. I began researching, reading and attending training sessions in an effort to understand the vehement emotion I had felt while standing over my newborn daughter's cot.

In my family, fate has placed an equals sign between love and death. A pattern of loss runs throughout my family history. My maternal grandmother was orphaned before she reached the age of nine. She was passed from one relative to another; as a young wife she lost two babies. My grandfather's early death then confirmed the thesis that everyone was leaving her. My paternal line was no more fortunate in this regard. My great-grandfather was born on 24 December 1882, three days after his father's death, while his grown-up brother was dying. His mother was half-mad with pain. There wasn't much prospect of her caring for the baby. Therefore the midwife decided to put the newborn next to the sick brother: maybe he'd catch the fatal disease and that would offer one resolution to the hopeless situation. My paternal grandmother was suddenly separated from her two brothers and her father due to her parents' divorce, with the result that she did not see them for years. Then the great love of her life died of pneumonia half a year after their wedding. She had two sons by her second husband, but lost one of them when he was one-and-a-half years old. Wherever I explore the family tree I stumble over losses. Over the years, not only people but land, wealth and successful businesses were included on this sad ledger of loss.

And what did all this mean in my life? It meant that I was afraid of any commitment and was careful lest I came to harm. I was afraid that I would very soon lose the person I came to love. It took a lot of therapy for the echoes of old traumas to fade and for me to realise that I didn't have to carry on the anxieties that my ancestors left to me. However, in order to do that I first had to delve into their stories.

Family script

Pick only so much from reality.
The symbolic moment of our weaknesses.
A feeble, ash-grey slice of life.
So everything that is a sign is our weapon
against time and space.
János Sziveri, '"A crack" – I think'[3]

In order to have as precise a view as possible of the inheritance our ancestors have passed to us, it is worth drawing up our family's genogram. A genogram is more than a family tree. While a family tree contains the bare facts, such as names and dates of birth and death, a genogram reveals the hidden depths of a family's past: it shows the emotional relations between family members, outlines recurrent patterns, and brings to the surface the family's unconscious manifestations. With its help we can reveal how even a distant ancestor's experience or trauma might be affecting our own fate.

Of course, we must not forget to map the relevant historical circumstances on to the social network shown

in the genogram. In order to uncover as precisely as possible what forces shaped the lives of our ancestors, it is
important to see what historical or economic changes
took place during their lifetime. The reactions to these
disclose a great deal about how we behave when we must
adapt to sudden changes.

When making a genogram the following information
is traditionally gathered and marked on a template:

— *Surnames, first names and nicknames of family
    members (pay attention to repetitions, the meaning of
    names and 'telling' nicknames)*
— *Changes of name (why were they changed and how did
    they affect the family?)*
— *Choosing a partner*
— *Dates of beginning and end of marriages and
    cohabitation*
— *Dates of birth*
— *Dates of death*
— *Adoption*
— *Emotional quality of relationships (close, fractious,
    broken off . . .)*
— *Excluded or rejected members of the family*
— *Previously unknown or hidden members of the family*
— *Acquired or hereditary diseases*
— *Accidents and their consequences*
— *Miscarriages and abortions*
— *Nationality*
— *Geographical location*

- *Moving or forced removal/resettlement*
- *Deportation*
- *Emigration*
- *Religion, possible changes of religion (when and why the change occurred)*
- *Education (what expectations were there in relation to studying?)*
- *Occupation*
- *Financial situation (date and reason of ensuing changes)*
- *Employment abroad*
- *Military service*
- *Retirement, working while retired*
- *Conflict with the law, criminal records, prison sentences (the nature of the crime)*
- *Physical abuse, incest, neglect between family members*
- *Smoking, alcohol and other drug addiction*
- *Present residence of family members*
- *Outside people who had an important role in the family's life (neighbours, friends, doctors, teachers, etc.)*
- *Important events that affected the family's life or caused a significant change*

If the dates of events can be discovered, they should be noted. Try to enquire about the reasons – for example, why a relative emigrated or changed religion, or what the reasons were for a divorce in the family.

After the data have been collected, draw up the genogram, the pictorial display of the family's history. Think over – or, better still, write down the answers to – the following questions:

- *What were your thoughts and feelings while you were making your family's genogram?*
- *What questions came up and what aspects were you unsure about?*
- *Was there anyone in the family you could discuss them with?*
- *How did the family members react to the collection of data?*
- *Did anyone express negative feelings about it or refuse to answer?*
- *Who offered most support making the genogram?*
- *Are there any blind spots in the history of the family?*
- *Are there any similarities in the difficulties experienced by different generations?*
- *How did different generations of the family tackle the difficulties they faced?*
- *What resources does your family have?*
- *What is the usual way of tackling difficulties?*
- *What are the recurring problems in the life of the family?*
- *How would you summarise in one sentence the family's message or motto for the next generation?*
- *What message do the lives of family members indicate?*
- *Which family member's fate had the greatest effect on you?*
- *What connections does the genogram help to reveal?*

— Can you see any repetitions and characteristically recurring patterns in your family with respect to relationships, personal histories, occupations, illnesses or accidents?

— Have any objects played an important role in the life of the family (for example, a house, a vineyard, a brooch belonging to a great-grandmother, a watch belonging to a grandfather, or a painting)?

Making a genogram and answering the questions at the end of the chapters in this book provide a solid basis for a deeper process of self-knowledge. Of course, you mustn't become exasperated if the information you have about your family history is insufficient or if you don't happen to know much about the lives of previous generations. A single name, a date or the name of a village where they once lived may often lead to the discovery of other missing details. In many cases it is not family members but old friends, neighbours and colleagues who can provide valuable information. It is also worth searching genealogy and family history websites: in Hungary, the Register Office's historical records from 1895 to 1980 are available online.

But what happens if despite all your efforts you don't succeed in learning anything about your family's past? Well, that in itself can be telling. Why might that be? Gaps in a family's history always betray interrupted or scanty, reserved relationships. You may have lost your parents early or perhaps you were brought up by adoptive parents. Perhaps nobody in the family ever deemed it important to talk about their lives or to share their experiences. If you struggle with insecurities in relationships and have difficulties with regard to attachment, the very lacunae in your family history can help you understand why, even if you don't find the traces of precise, relevant details. Your own troubles, characteristic reactions and recurring patterns of behaviour are not all about you but also about the lives of your ancestors, even if you are unable to discover anything about them.

As an example, let's consider the life of a world-famous and rather extraordinary man. We can do so without compunction since he himself always said that as far as he was concerned there were no taboos in his life, that nothing was off-limits: one could ask him anything and whatever he knew, he would share. In relating his life story, we can reflect on how the topics of the chapters of this book can be traced in his fate.

Steven Paul Jobs – known the world over as Steve Jobs – was one of the most dynamic figures of recent decades.[4] The former CEO of Apple was variously called an infernal computing genius, a brilliant inventor, a creative manager, an arrogant jerk, and a cruel and narcissistic loner who took advantage of others. But who really was he? This man, who through his devices is still very much part of our lives – what was his background, where did he come from?

*

Steve Jobs's mother was Joanne Carole Schieble, the daughter of a Catholic family of German descent. His father, Abdulfattah 'John' Jandali, was the son of a wealthy Syrian Muslim family who had arrived in the United States as a political refugee. His parents met and fell in love at the University of Wisconsin where Jandali was an assistant lecturer while Schieble was in her final year studying speech therapy. Schieble's strict Catholic parents were not too happy about the relationship. Moreover, when the 23-year-old woman became pregnant, her father threatened to disown her if she married Jandali – so she decided instead to give her future baby up for adoption. About the child's adoptive parents, she had only one condition: they must be college graduates. A lawyer and his wife were originally chosen, but when they learned that the child, born on 24 February 1955, was a boy and not the girl they desired, they walked away. There was a bit of a snag with the next couple on the waiting list as they had not even finished secondary-school education. According to reports, Joanne Schieble spent weeks ruminating what to do and kept putting off signing the official adoption papers. In the end she agreed to the adoption on condition that the couple would provide for the child's education and set aside the university fees in a separate bank account from the beginning. The adoptive parents did as promised, yet Steve Jobs did not even complete his first year of university because he found most of the classes so boring. However, since his lecturers were aware of his outstanding abilities, they allowed him to attend freely whatever courses interested him. In this, as in so much else, Jobs was inventive and did not care a fig for rules.

Let's pause here and take stock of how Steve Jobs started his life. His conception was not planned; moreover, its announcement aroused definite aversion in his future grandfather. With such a start, we can presume that his mother was often distressed during the months of her pregnancy. When it became clear that she would have to decide between her child and her family, her tension probably increased. As we saw in the first chapter, stress hormones in a mother's body influence the formation of the nervous system in the embryo, causing structural and functional changes which will later affect the child's physical and psychological development.

Let's note another important factor: by the time Steve Jobs was born, he had already been given up by not one but two families: his biological mother let him go (while trying to ensure the best possible future for him) and the lawyer couple originally chosen as adoptive parents withdrew because of the baby's sex. Of course, these facts do not reach a newborn baby, but the baby can nevertheless sense tension developing all around. Although it's worth treating her words with due caution, one of Jobs's future girlfriends said in an interview that he was never quite able to ignore the experience of rejection that was encoded as a fundamental motif in his inner world.

According to other reports, Jobs had difficulty fitting

in at school, too: like many unwanted children, he was often mocked, bullied and ostracised. Is it possible that his classmates sensed the initial injury of his life and so chose him as a target for bullying? Is it possible that peer-group dynamics characterising unwanted children were dominant when he was at school?

It is also worth considering whether there's any connection between Jobs's early experiences of rejection and his strange habits. Friends and colleagues recall that in his youth Jobs followed a strict diet for many months, eating nothing but fruit, vegetables and seeds. So convinced was he that the diet was beneficial for his body that he did not feel the need to wash himself. However, his colleagues were of a quite different opinion and therefore they soon had to ask him to work only at night so that he wouldn't bother anyone with his body odour. The care we take, including with our body, reveals much about our deepest relationship with ourselves. Is it possible that Jobs's strict diet and neglect of personal hygiene signalled a lack of self-love? Could an unconscious self-destructive mindset have played a role in his decisions, as is the case with so many unwanted children? Another telling incident: Jobs's health was already in such a poor state and his immune system so weakened that he needed to be shielded against the most insignificant infections – but when his doctor asked him to put on a mask, he refused, saying that he did not like its design.

Now let's look at Jobs's noted perfectionism. The Apple CEO's adoptive father, Paul Reinhold Jobs, was a brilliant handyman with superb craftsmanship. Later on, Jobs often said that his meticulous eye and way of working had been absorbed from hours of tinkering beside his father in the workshop that was set up in the garage. However, perfectionism is not merely a learned behaviour: the drive to be perfect most often derives from a deep sense of internal insufficiency. In order to avoid the attendant sense of shame, a perfectionist does their utmost to meet expectations primarily set by themselves. For such a person, acceptable means flawless. Might Jobs's famous mania for perfection be another symptom of his early experience of rejection? Was he, perhaps, driven by an unconscious desire to prove his own value and ultimately overwrite his difficult start in life? Of course, there are no definite answers; one can only speculate about the possibilities.

One thing is beyond doubt: the modern world watched with fascination as each new Mac and iPhone was launched on to the market, and the majority of consumers have had a deep and almost intimate attachment to the company's products. Jobs, whose security of attachment was already shaken in the embryonic period, practically chained people to the objects he made. When, puzzled, I once asked someone about this almost magnetic attraction, they told me, 'You know, having an Apple device is more than having a certain type of computer: it also means you belong to a family. Wherever you are, your fellow Apple owners smile and look on you as a brother.' That really makes me think. A man whose biological parents could not bring him up on account of pressure from their family created products that awaken in their users an unprecedented, deep, and almost primal, experience of belonging.

By the way, Jobs's biological parents got married after Joanne Schieble's father's death, and their second child, the novelist Mona Simpson, was born shortly afterwards. Jobs only learned about his biological sister after managing to find his mother in adulthood. Mona asked Jobs to find their father, who by then had left her too, but Jobs refused: he did not want to know anything of his father.

Jobs himself became a father at the age of twenty-three – precisely the same age as his own parents had been when he was born. However, he only took the child on in name many years later following a conclusive DNA test. Their relationship was never close, and his daughter claims still to carry the painful memory of rejection . . . as if fate were repeating itself. Jobs's ambivalence is indicated by the fact that despite his long denial of his daughter's existence, he later named his first computer, Lisa, after her.

Professionally, Steve Jobs created something extra-ordinary. His colleagues, who on many occasions tried in vain to explain why his ideas could not be realised, remember him as someone who had a special 'reality distortion field'. Getting close to him, the impossible became possible.

Throughout his life, Jobs defied reality. He is an iconic figure, an inspiration for generations – yet despite his astounding success in the world of technology and business, in his closest relationships he was wounded and caused wounds. Shortly before his death, he said the following:

I want to believe that something endures . . . after you die . . . Maybe, that's just like an on–off switch. Click, you're off. You're gone. It's over. Maybe that's why I didn't like to put on–off switches on Apple devices. Now I know . . . other things would be needed that don't have anything to do with wealth. Something far more important. Perhaps relationships, perhaps art, perhaps the dreams of our youth . . . Life isn't limited. Go where you want to! Reach the height you want to! Everything's there in your heart and hands.

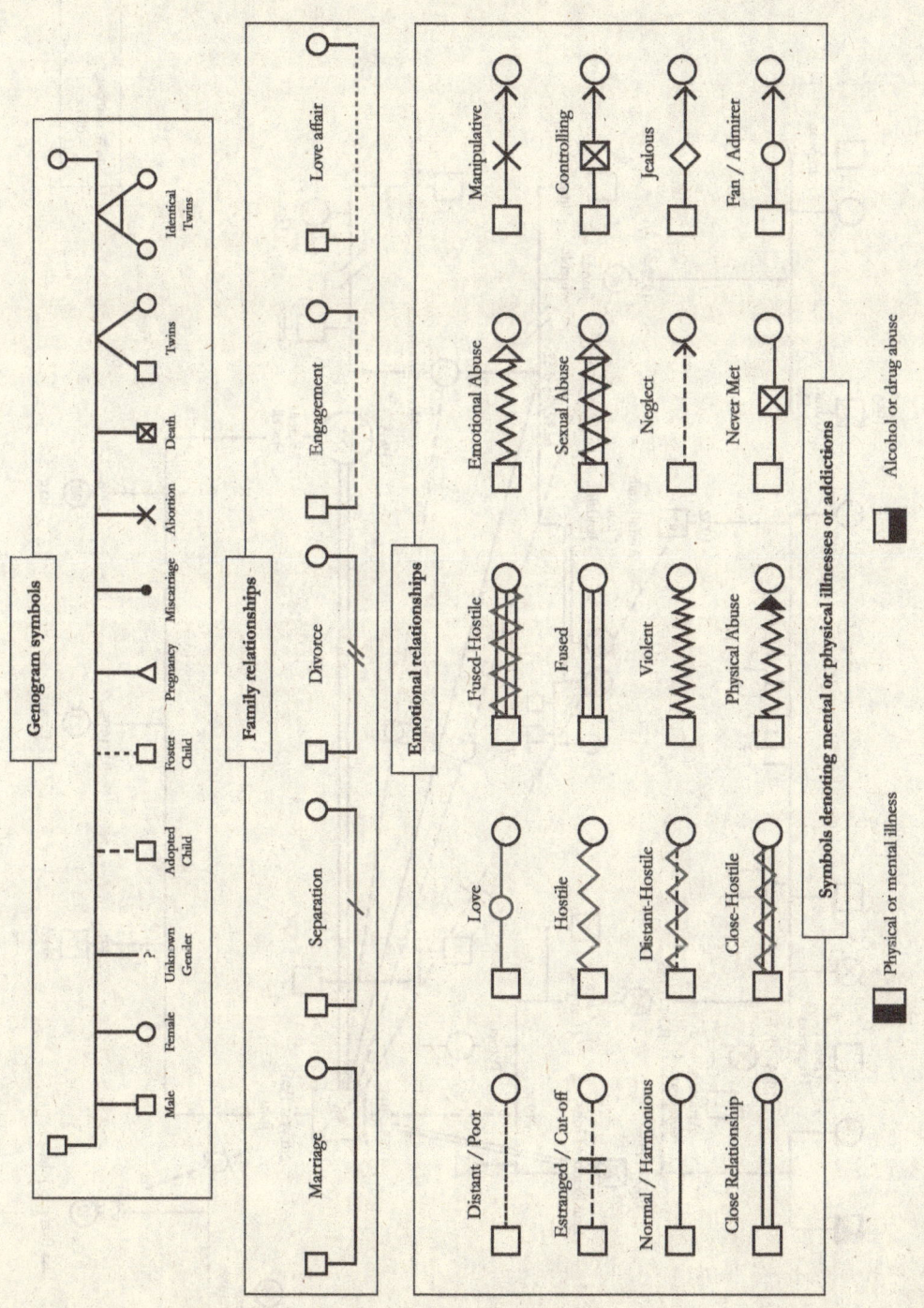

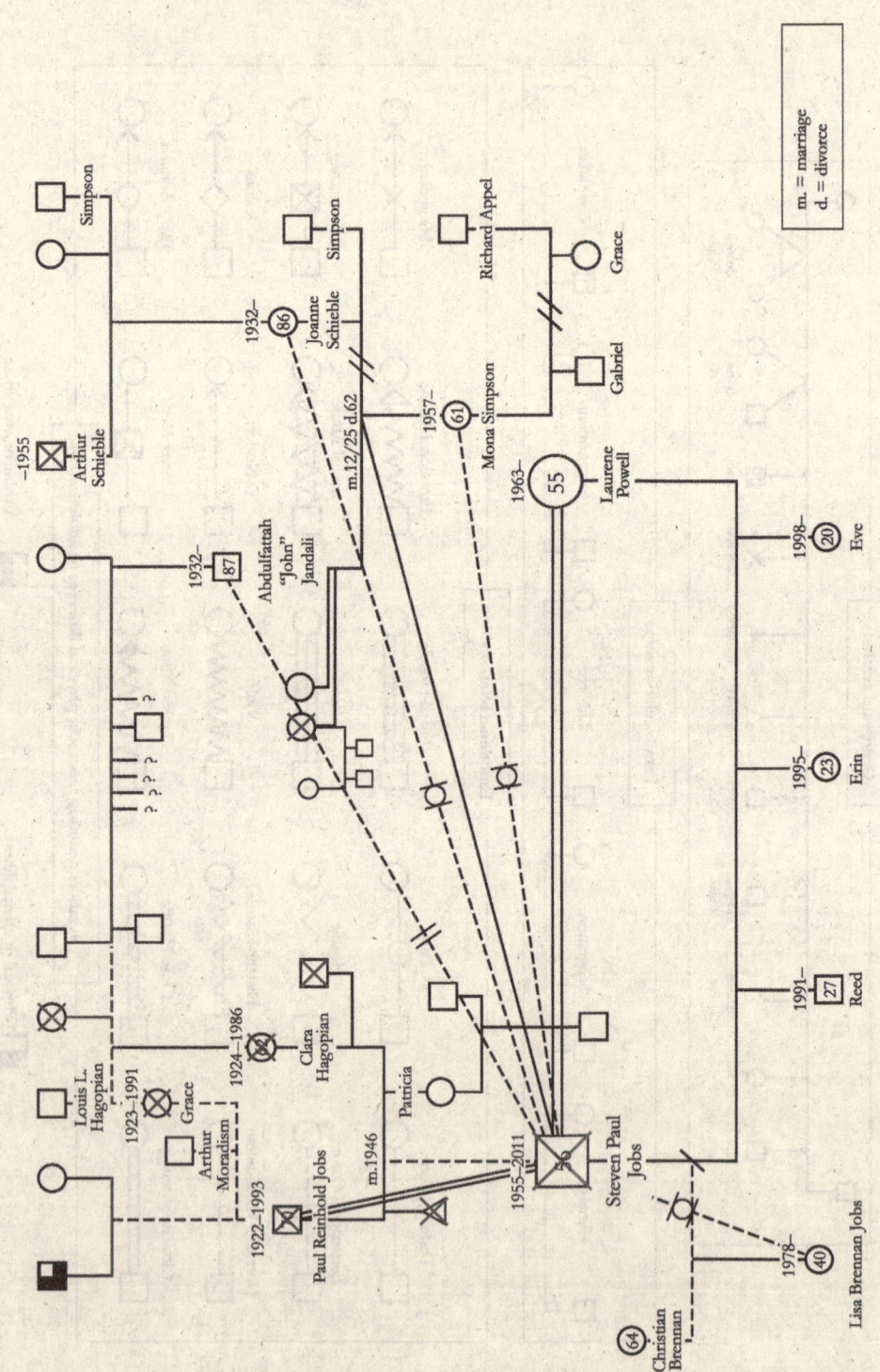

m. = marriage
d. = divorce

Afterword

When is a book ready? When can we lean back, satisfied we have said everything we wanted to say, everything that matters, about a certain topic? I don't think that moment ever comes. Our theme is almost infinite: whichever way we turn, it offers new possibilities and helps explore new connections. Just as there is no finished self-knowledge, I must realise, neither is there a finished book: there is only an arbitrary end point – and the hope that the reader will find a thread that leads them finally to begin to relieve themselves of the burdens of the unprocessed past and shape their fate consciously and freely. I don't know any journey more exciting than that of self-knowledge. We may travel to distant, exotic countries, we may come to know extraordinary cultures – but the discoveries that await us in our own inner world hold realisations that are incomparable.

If we set about exploring the hitherto hidden layers of our personality, we'll definitely need one thing: patience. However earnestly we seek to understand connections, overcome ingrained habits and make progress, change does not happen like a flash of lightning. While a single therapeutic conversation can be enough to reveal certain causes and effects, deeper transformations of personality require patient, careful attention.

Notes

1. How it began

1 Attila József (1905–37), *Nagyon Fáj* (Budapest, CSerep-falvi, 1936).

2 The original title of the song is 'Ha előrelátó csecsemő lettél volna', from the album *Százbolha* by Sziámi (2009), lyrics by Péter Müller and János Gasner.

3 Péter Popper, *Lélekrágcsálók – válogatás Popper Péter legjobb előadásaiból* (*Gnawing at the Soul: A Selection of Péter Popper's Best Lectures*) (Budapest: Kulcslyuk Kiadó, 2010).

4 See https://www.frontiersin.org/articles/10.3389/fnbeh. 2021.706660/full

5 Originally in German, 'Das unwillkommene Kind und sein Todestrieb', *IZP*, 1929 (XV: 149–53) and published in the same year in English as 'The Unwelcome Child and his Death-Instinct', *International Journal of Psycho-Analysis*, 1929 (X: 125–9).

6 Helga Häsing and Ludwig Janus, *Ungewollte Kinder* (Berlin: Rowohlt Verlag, 1994).

7 Andrew Feldmár, *Rainbow States of Consciousness* (Budapest: Jaffa Kiadó, 2010).

8 H. P. David, Z. Matějček and Z. Dytrych, 'Born Unwanted: Observations from the Prague Study', *American Psychologist*, 2003 (58(3): 224–9).

9 György Petri (1943–2000). Translated by Dóra Elekes.

10 Péter Popper, op. cit.

11 Carl Gustav Jung, 'Paracelsus as a Spiritual Phenomenon' (1929), trans. R. F. C. Hull, in *The Spirit in Man, Art, and Literature*, Vol. 15 of the *Collected Works*, ed. Herbert Read, Michael Fordham and Gerhard Adler (London: Routledge, 2014), p. 4.

12 Salvador Dalí, *The Secret Life of Salvador Dalí*, trans. Haakon M. Chevalier (New York: Dover Publications, 1993), p. 201.

13 *Ibid.*, p. 152.

14 Quote attributed to Albert Schweitzer (1875–1965), German and French musician, theologian and physician.

15 Kevin Leman, *The Birth Order Book* (Grand Rapids, MI: Revell/Baker Publishing Group, 2nd edn, 1998, repr. 2009).

2. *Trauma*

1 Aristotle, *De Anima* (*On the Soul*), trans. E. M. Edghill with minor emendations by Daniel Kolak (Book I, Ch. 1), p. 3 (available at https://antilogicalism.com/wp-content/uploads/2016/12/aristotle_anima_final.pdf).

2 Ludmila Ulitskaya, *Daniel Stein, Interpreter*, trans. Arch Tait (London: Overlook Duckworth, Peter Mayer, 2011), p. 61.

3 Judith Herman, *Trauma and Recovery* (London: Rivers Oram Press, 1994).

4 Bruno Bettelheim, *Surviving and Other Essays* (New York: Alfred A. Knopf, 1979), p. 14.

5 Hanscarl Leuner, *Katathym-imaginative Psychotherapie* (Stuttgart: Thieme, 1994); *A katatím imaginatív pszichoterápia alapjai* (Budapest: Animula Kiadó, 2012).

6 Árpád Tóth (1886–1928), 'The Rhythm of the Ancestors'. Translated by Dóra Elekes.

7 Richard Dawkins, *The Selfish Gene* (Oxford: Oxford University Press, 2006), p. 35.

8 https://docplayer.hu/159349-Epigenetika-a-biologiai-mukodes-szoftvere-falus-andras-osszefoglalas.html

9 Éva Péterfy-Novák, *Apád előtt ne vetkőzz* (Budapest: Libri, 2019).

10 Alice Miller, *For Your Own Good*, trans. Hildegarde and Hunter Hannum (New York: Macmillan, 2002).

11 Szilárd Borbély, *Nincstelenek* (Budapest: Kalligram Kiadó, 2013).

12 Lance Morrow, *Heart* (Alfred A. Knopf/Knopf Canada, 2003), p. 240.

13 Alaine Polcz, *Asszony a fronton* (Budapest: Jelenkor, 2021).

14 Andrea Pető, *Elmondani az elmondhatatlant: a nemi erőszak története Magyarországon a II. világháború alatt* (Budapest: Jaffa, 2018).

15 Albert Camus, *The Fall*, trans. Justin O'Brien, 1957 (London: Vintage Books, 1991), p. 34.

16 M. W. Baldwin and B. Fehr, 'On the instability of attachment style ratings', *Personal Relationships*, 1995 (2 (3): 247–61); E. Waters, S. Merrick, D. Treboux, J. Crowell and L. Albersheim, 'Attachment security in infancy and early adulthood: a twenty-year longitudinal study', *Child Development*, 2000 (71(3): 684–9); L. Kirkpatrick and C. Hazen,

'Attachment styles and close relationships: A four-year prospective study', *Personal Relationships*, 1994 (1(2): 123–42); Péter Fónagy, 'A kötődés generációs átvitele: Egy új elmélet', *Thalassa*, 2003 (2–3: 83–106).

17 Marinus H. van IJzendoorn, 'Adult attachment representations, parental responsiveness, and infant attachment: a meta-analysis on the predictive validity of the Adult Attachment Interview', *Psychological Bulletin*, 1995 (117(3): 387).

18 József Kármán, *Fanni hagyományai* (Budapest: Magvető Publishers, 1978).

19 An adaptation of the autobiographically inspired novels of that name by Edward St Aubyn (London: Picador, 2018).

3. Family secrets

1 Fyodor Dostoevsky, *The Brothers Karamazov*, trans. Richard Pevear and Larissa Volokhonsky (London: Vintage Classics, 1991), p. 255.

2 Haruki Murakami, *Sputnik Sweetheart*, trans. Philip Gabriel (London: Vintage, 2002), p. 153.

3 Gerard Martin, *Gabriel García Márquez: A Life* (London: Vintage, 2008), p. 228.

4 Ádám Bodor, *Az értelmezés útvesztői* (*Labyrinths of Interpretation*) (Budapest: Magvető Kiadó, 2021).

5 Friedrich Nietzsche, *The Antichrist*, trans. Antony M. Ludovici (Ware: Wordsworth Editions, 2007), p. 144.

6 András Cserna-Szabó, *Az abbé a fejével játszik* (Budapest: Helikon, 2018).

7 Voltaire, *Candide and Other Stories*, trans. Roger Pearson (Oxford: Oxford University Press, 2006), p. 53.

8 Carl R. Rogers, *On Becoming a Person: A Therapist's View of Psychotherapy* (Boston: Houghton Mifflin, 1961), p. 26.

4. Forming the family's fate

1 Thomas Nagel, *The Last Word* (Oxford: Oxford University Press, 2001), p. 1.

2 Krisztián Grecsó, *Isten hozott* (Budapest: Magvető Publishing, 2005).

3 Mihaly Csikszentmihalyi, *Flow* (New York: Harper Perennial Modern Classics, 2008), p. 177.

4 Bruno Bettelheim, *A Good Enough Parent* (New York: Random House, 1988).

5 Salvador Minuchin, *Families and Family Therapy* (Cambridge, MA: Harvard University Press, 1974), p. 58.

6 Thomas Mann, *Doctor Faustus*, trans. John E. Woods (New York: Vintage International, 1999), p. 236.

7 Barry Lopez, *Crow and Weasel* (New York: Farrar, Straus and Giroux (North Point Press), 1990).

8 Vilmos Csányi, *Íme, az ember. A humánetológus szemével* (Budapest: Libri, 2015).

9 Annamária Kádár, *Mesepszichológia a gyakorlatban* (Budapest: Kulcslyuk Publishing, 2017).

10 Mihály Babits, 'A humanizmus és korunk' ('Humanism and our Age'), in *Esszék, tanulmányok*, Vol. 2 (Budapest: Szépirodalmi Kiadó, 1978).

5. In the wake of inheritance

1 Agatha Christie, *4:50 from Paddington*, (London, 1957, William Collins).
2 Ferenc Birtalan (1945–2018), 'Inheritance'. Translated by Dóra Elekes.
3 János Sziveri, (1954–1990), originally published as '"*Rés*" – *gondolom*', *The Complete Poems of János Sziveri* (Budapest, Kortárs Folyóirat Kiadói Kft, 1994).
4 Walter Isaacson, *Steve Jobs* (Budapest: HVG Könyvek, 2011). Besides Walter Isaacson's biography, I used several online sources to present Steve Jobs's life story, which I supplemented with my own subjective analysis.

Acknowledgements

I thank my teachers for allowing me to learn from them: Prof. Dr Katalin Varga, who taught me so much about the importance of the foetal and perinatal period; and Dr Ildikó Kuritárné Szabó, for making me aware of the long-term effects of trauma. I am grateful for the works of Bessel van der Kolk, Peter Levine and Judith Herman, among others, which have shaped my perspective. I thank my editor and agent, Bence Sárközy, for believing in me and paving the way for the book's international publication.

Last but not least, I thank my family, especially my daughter Olivia, for giving me the time to write the book and for putting up with me when the world was closing in on my laptop keyboard. Thank you for the evolutionary journey we have been on together, and thank you for allowing me to experience four generations coming together to heal transgenerational traumas. Thank you to my grandmothers, my mother and my daughter for being open and brave, for daring to face the past and all the pain. Thank you for the tears and the hugs, and thank you for staying the course.